JON WHYTE
MIND OVER MOUNTAINS

Y0-ACG-472

JON WHYTE

MIND OVER MOUNTAINS

edited by Harry Vandervlist

RED DEER PRESS

All rights reserved. No part of this book may be reproduced by any means, electronic or mechanical, including photography, recording, or any information storage and retrieval system, without permission in writing from the publisher.

Thanks are due many people, but especially Harry Vandervlist, University of Calgary, for taking up this editorial challenge; Myrna Kostash for the foreword; Douglas Leonard, Executive Director, Whyte Museum of the Canadian Rockies, for supplying financial assistance; Sally Truss, Manager, Marketing and Development, Whyte Museum of the Canadian Rockies, for coordinating project research and promotion; Craig Richards for the generous contribution of photography; Shela Shapiro and Kristi Baron, Marketing and Development Assistants, Whyte Museum of the Canadian Rockies; Don Bourdon, Head Archivist, Lena Goon, Archives Assistant, and Elisabeth Kundert, Librarian, Whyte Museum of the Canadian Rockies, for research assistance.

RED DEER PRESS
Room 813, MacKimmie Library Tower
2500 University Drive NW
Calgary Alberta Canada T2N 1N4

Cover and book design by Duncan Campbell
Front cover photo by Edward Cavell
Back cover photo by Pam Knott
Interior photos by Craig Richards
Printed by Houghton-Boston Lithographers, Saskatoon, Canada, for Red Deer Press

Financial support provided by the Whyte Museum of the Canadian Rockies, the Alberta Foundation for the Arts, a beneficiary of the Lottery Fund of the Government of Alberta, and by the Canada Council, the Department of Canadian Heritage and the University of Calgary.

Canadian Cataloguing in Publication Data

Whyte, Jon, 1941–1991.
Jon Whyte

Poems.
ISBN 0-88995-204-3 (bound)— ISBN 0-88995-208-6 (pbk.)

I. Vandervlist, Harry, 1961– II. Title. III. Title: Mind over mountains.
PS8595.H95J66 2000   C811'.54 C00-910201-9
PR9199.3.W459J66 2000

5 4 3 2 1

UNIVERSITY LIBRARY
UNIVERSITY OF ALBERTA

CONTENTS

INVENTING *the* CANADIAN ROCKIES

FOREWORD

I watched Jon Whyte from the sidelines, the geeky poet with the pretzel for a body—and how he walked pelvis first, the rest of his torso following later—lank hair, spectacles, bad teeth, books under arm. He sat of a morning in the booth kitty-corner from mine at the Tuck Shop, near the campus of the University of Alberta, where a group of his friends and associates (as I thought enviously of them), were already waiting for him. It was probably winter because whenever I flash back to this scene, I see bodies pressed together in the swaddling layers of furry and shaggy jackets and coats, in some modern version of bundling, before the Sexual Revolution hit. The mom and pop who ran the café had passed through with the coffee pot, pouring it with gusto into thick white china cups (the kind with the green stripe running around under the rim) and soon would be bearing trays of fresh hot cinnamon buns to our tables. We could smell the spices and melting brown sugar on the air.

Years later Jon Whyte would propose a book to the board of NeWest Press to be called *The Cinnamon Bun Years,* but the board was never persuaded this would fly beyond the local market for nostalgia. You had to have been there. Otherwise it didn't mean anything, these last few moments of Edmonton's youthful intelligentsia before the Sixties came to town (which was in 1965, give or take a year) and became the only story that people would want to tell later. Those wintery mornings in the Tuck Shop were 1963, 1964, when I was an undergraduate at the university, freshly minted from an Edmonton high school, brainy in sensible shoes, unsexed by a bad haircut and pleated plaid skirts, a bluestocking after her time, a secret poet, encumbered by the friendship of similarly lacklustre 18-year-olds studying Modern Languages. I longed to be elsewhere. I imagined France and Moscow and Greenwich Village. But right then, on that whited-out snowy morning on the prairies, the booth of Jon Whyte and his friends in the Tuck Shop would do.

They were bohemians. That's how I thought of them. Men in beards, women in long loose hair, wearing turtlenecks, smoking Balkan cigarettes, reading their poems to one another and joining their voices to those of the New York and San Francisco beats. Did Mel Hurtig already have his bookstore downtown? Is that where I bought *Howl* and *Coney Island of the Mind?* They listened to jazz on CKUA and wrote book reviews for *Gateway,* the campus newspaper. They drank Chianti and espresso. They quoted dialogue from black-and-white Italian films. They sat in the curved booth in each other's arms and laughed. I wanted to be with them. I wanted to be them.

I left Edmonton in 1965 and didn't come back for ten years. I returned a writer, and that is probably the reason why, of that whole magical milieu I have conjured up from memory and fantasy, it is Jon Whyte in particular I see among its faded figures. For it was Jon whom I would meet up with, by then a fellow writer, a published scribe, who like me had decided to settle down at his sources (Banff, in his case) and commit his mind and heart to the challenge of recreating homeplace as a literary subject. That's how we met again, as equals, as compatriots, as collaborators. It was to prove a joy.

I had visited Banff since my childhood in the 1950s on summer holidays with my parents, who rented cabins on Muskrat Avenue and took us to swim at the grand pool of Cave and Basin and to hike up wild Johnson's Canyon. Gone, all gone. By the time I ran into Jon again in the late 1970s, this Banff had been dismantled in favour of serious international tourism. He had watched it happen, and it was only I who was surprised, even aghast, to find him in a smart Italian restaurant on Banff Avenue, holding court at his table near the front. "Hello," he said, mischievously. "Won't you join me and my friends for supper?" Jon Whyte was hailing me to his table! He seemed thoroughly at ease, not minding this bit of urban chic in his beloved national park. Maybe this was even how one ought to live, as a cosmopolitan who knew his Tuscan merlots, collected chess sets from Tibet, hiked up Kilimanjaro and always came back home to continue as a poet, book designer, journalist and museum curator, poring over the exquisite details of the terrain underfoot, historical and geophysical and mythological, love at close quarters—not even minding how the Paris Cafe had changed, enjoying his lunches there, even if the waitresses in black frocks with white aprons and caps, striding smartly over the waxed floorboards, had vanished.

It is time to turn back; time to turn from the mysteries; the hunt is over. At the sun's rising my shadow yearned itself into the tall grass: At noon my shadow was short; I was unaware of my shadow: Now in the dusk my shadow stretches and points toward home: We will rise and walk early into the sun with the sun behind us when day is done. About the lone bear at the edge of the woods who nudged a stump over to eat its grub a noose of the sun tightens. . . .

He wrote in *Homage, Henry Kelsey* in 1981—a kind of riff-by-noun-and-verb, in syncopation with that first white storyteller of those parts, Henry Kelsey of the Hudson's Bay Company in his journal, "If god permits me for one two years space, the Inland Country of Good report hath been by Indians but by English yet not seen." This "collab-oration" that began in 1967 as a poem about muskoxen gave me his set of eyes to look at home and see it new again.

I would see him too in the log home of the Whytes, Catharine and Peter alongside the Whyte Museum, cata-loguing and narrating the artefacts of the lives and passions that had engen-dered his. Or standing straight as a spear in the old cemetery of Banff on Remembrance Day, wrapped by a nasty wind, enjoying hugely his task as raconteur of the lives gone down to their graves. Or beaming back at me from the audience in the lodge at Radium Hot Springs the last summer of his life. It looks grim, he told us at coffee break, of the results of a medi-cal exam. But he was grinning at me, this kindred spirit. He was saying hello, here's looking at you, kid, and he was saying goodbye, stepping out

of the circle where he had held a place for me.

We worked together on the council and executive of the Writers Guild of Alberta (he was veep to my presi-dent, and then took the presidency himself in 1990) because he under-stood that artists do not spring fully armed from the foreheads of the gods but struggle their way through history and society, not to mention (risible amounts of) money. He kept on writing newspaper columns—with real dash and withering indig-nation—to remind his readers that we live in circles of commitment to one another and all living things, and that the language of commerce and self-interest impoverishes our speech if it holds a monopoly. He was the complete citizen, and it is our collective loss that he does not still live among us, a tribune of the common interest as the fate of our wild lands falls increasingly into the hands of developers of golf courses.

I am a child of the parkland and after a period of time in Banff, I always begin to fret at the feeling of rigid enclosure inside the vice of the encircling mountains, and I long for the breakaway of the horizon. But I

know that Jon did not feel that way. He lived in a landscape that was pro-tean and vivid with sounds and motions—wind and rivers and stone—and that was re-created clean and whole and ideal through his prodigious pleasure with language as well as sensation.

Hail, Kelsey, come: the land is not bar-ren, land of little sticks, caribou lichen, musketers only; come to the land: the land is not barren, the land that is mused, is browsed, is fused by moose-ways over, among, between, and through the muskrat-slickened banks of oozing mud. . . . The land is not barren; the glaciers' scores on the rusty rock reveal that life withdrew but has returned. . . .

I stand at Jon's grave in the old town cemetery and look around me, chat-ting all the while, hoping he is pleased to have a visitor. But it is all I can do to manage a tone of con-viviality, for I am in a towering rage that hasn't abated since the morning I learned of his death the night before. It was expected—indeed, I had last seen him just a couple of weeks earlier, in his hospital room, when he talked of Venice, but halt-ingly and dreamily, so I knew he was leaving us, and our lives were already becoming his memory—but the rage is justified nevertheless. For of all the people I know, Jon was the one who most hugely enjoyed his own life—books, friends, conversation, wordplay, dictionaries, food, treks, beasts, ghosts, lore—so much so that his joy spilled over into the lives of any who drew near him. When Jon died I felt that I had irrevocably lost some capacity to live at a certain pitch of appetite whose excitements he had been the first to display all those years ago in a campus coffee house.

He died too young, he deserved more time, he was hauled away in the middle of a thought, a passion, a meal, and we will never know what it was he was about to tell us, show us, summon us to. The rage is for the infuriating incompletion of a big life out of the ordinary. He would have made an extraordinary old man. Let us imagine him.

MYRNA KOSTASH
JUNE 2000

INTRODUCTION

Born in Banff in 1941, Jon Whyte was variously a bookseller, editor, book designer, arts journalist, film-maker, local historian, environmentalist, traveller and museumologist—but above all he was a pioneering poet who experimented with style and language in order to capture the landscapes of the Canadian Rockies. It might be more accurate to say that he worked at rescuing those landscapes from beneath the layers of cliché that make it difficult to see them in a fresh or even a visionary way. Jon, who did experience the Rockies in a visionary way, believed that experience ran in two directions. On one hand, artists actually create the landscape around them, so that what we call Lake Louise was not discovered but "invented." Yet at the same time as we shape our perceptions of the mountains with our words, paint or photographs, the mountains also shape us.

Jon was certainly shaped by the experience of growing up on the banks of the Bow River. He lived in Banff until he was fifteen, and except for the period between 1956 and 1968, Banff remained his home for life. During those years away, Jon completed high school in Medicine Hat and then spent his university years in Edmonton. Completing a B.A. in 1964, Jon remained at the University of Alberta to teach creative writing, work as a broadcaster at the college radio station, CKUA, and write a Master's thesis on the medieval poem *The Pearl*. He went on to study at Stanford, but by 1968 he was back in Banff for good, and it was there that he completed his Stanford M.A. in Communications with his thesis film on Banff's legendary mountain man, Jimmy Simpson.

The Bow Valley gave Jon Whyte the geographical and spiritual roots needed to balance his mercurial and wide-ranging intellect. Jon was a true mental traveller, and all of his reading and teaching and conversation were passionately conducted. Over the course of his career, he fell in love again and again with ideas, with facts, with histories. This passion bore fruit in his work as an arts reporter for CBC Radio, a weekly columnist for Banff's *Crag and Canyon,* and an editor of well over a dozen works of local history. Whether writing about John Cage's music or Julian Jaynes's theory of the mind, John Hollander's concrete poems, Murray Schafer's music, Christo's Running Fence or Carl Rungius's big-game paintings, Jon ceaselessly made connections and created imaginative structures—in other words, he learned in a poetic and visionary fashion, shaping information into worlds.

As a poet Jon created his imaginative universe in words, but not only in words. He told Joan Murray in a 1977 interview that "at the age of thirteen or fourteen, when we're supposed to be completely turned off by the idea of poetry and not devote any time to it whatsoever in class, I was still taking secret delight and pleasure in it." He recalls "luxuriating in sweet sensuous sibilants" and "delighting in poetic paradox and the ways words have of generating their own meaningful nonsense, as in Lewis Carroll."

Yet at the same time, Jon had been immersed in visual culture from birth. His aunt and uncle, Peter and Catharine Whyte, lived a few doors from his house in Banff.

Peter and Catharine, both painters, had enormous influence on their nephew, and it's clear he looked at pictures and printed pages as carefully as he listened to words. Jon's books on painting and photography include *The Peter and Catharine Robb Whyte Portfolio, Carl Rungius: Painter of the Western Wilderness, Great Days in the Rockies: The Photography of Byron Harmon,* and *John Davenall Turner: Sunfield Painter* (the latter won the Wilfred Eggleston Award from the Writers Guild of Alberta). Every book Jon wrote or edited manifested his interest in book design, layout and typography.

So it's no surprise to see that the pages of Jon's poetry speak to readers not just in words, but through the language of spacing, typography and design as well. His years as a radio announcer taught Jon the power of voice, and he was proud of the performance skills he brought to live or recorded readings of his work. But given a blank page rather than a silent room, he was likely to treat the page as a canvas. He also wanted to set himself apart from poetry that he saw as too personal or relying too much on sentiment. Too many poets of his time, he complained, had read the Black Mountain poets or Margaret Atwood's poetry—but read them badly. Jon believed that poetry needed an architecture, an impersonal structure. For him those things could be found in history and in design. His imaginative work in these areas led poet and critic Eli Mandel to write in *Poetry Canada Review* that Jon Whyte had become by the mid-1980s "one of the two outstanding radical innovators in Canadian poetry" (along with Ontario poet Christopher Dewdney).

It was in the 1980s that Jon's poetic career really flourished. An early version of *Homage, Henry Kelsey* had appeared as early as 1971, and he continued to explore the potential of western historical subjects with *The Agony of Mrs. Stone,* which appeared in the journal *Matrix* in 1977. But 1981 saw the appearance of both the final version of *Homage, Henry Kelsey* and the collection entitled *Gallimaufry*. From then on, most of Jon's poetic energy went into his projected five-volume poem on the Rockies, of which two volumes appeared in his lifetime: *The Fells of Brightness, Vol. 1: Some Fittes and Starts* (1983) and *The Fells of Brightness, Vol. 2: Wenkchemna* (1985). Before his death in 1992 Jon completed one further installment of this project, a poem for radio entitled *Minisniwapta: Voices of the River.* The final poem is a collage of voices, sounds and historic texts, "both quoted and deconstructed," as Jon wrote in his own description of the work.

Although most of Jon's poetic work is concerned with writing the West, and the mountains, there were other sides to his imagination. He wrote for children (and admired Dennis Lee's success with *Alligator Pie)* and hoped to produce a book of children's verse. He spent months travelling in Asia with his aunt Catharine, and in Africa with his friend Pamela Knott, and he put many of these experiences into narrative poetry: "Alma Ata" is one example of his travel poetry.

As a professional writer and editor, he always had many projects under way and constantly proposed new ones. The result is the usual abundance of unfinished, abandoned or rejected work that active writers leave behind them. The work chosen for this collection, however, mainly reflects writing for which Jon was known and admired during his lifetime: *Homage, Henry Kelsey,* for example, won the Writers Guild of Alberta Stephan G. Stephansson Award in 1983. Of the poems collected here, "Ike Mills' Finishing School" has not, to my knowledge, appeared in print. The children's poem "Dinosaurs Mean So Much to Morris" and "The Agony of Mrs. Stone" have not previously appeared in book form.

The research for this book meant spending most of a summer in Banff, which is still a pleasant prospect, despite the many changes to that small town, changes Jon deplored in his weekly columns. But the most striking aspect of the time spent there was the realization that eight years after his death, Jon Whyte remains a vivid presence in Banff in the memories of his many friends and colleagues. A small aside in conversation or the discovery of an old

photo in the archives is still enough to revive memories of specific conversations with Jon. There's no question he became a guiding spirit in Banff from the late 1960s to the 1990s, when it began to shed the last of its Edwardian tourist-village isolation and turn itself into a meaningful centre for artists. To be honest, the warmth and fervour of ongoing appreciation for Jon Whyte surprised and at first embarrassed me, arriving like an outsider, an editor charged with revisiting Jon's papers and his poetic legacy for the purposes of this book. The feeling of trespassing at a stranger's wake, however, soon vanished, partly because studying Jon's writing made him less of a stranger and partly because his friends in Banff showed such generosity in helping make the book possible.

My hope is that this collection will map the warmth, generosity and imagination of a great man whose name has justifiably become synonymous with the Canadian Rockies.

WHEN THE WORLD was FIVE YEARS OLD

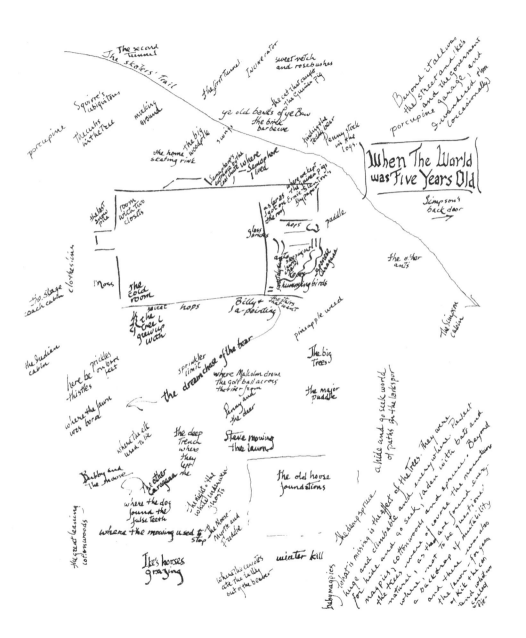

I've always lived
across the street
from wherever
I was going
Ike Mills' Riding School
the library
or the university
as close as
across the street
far enough away
to shape the difference
in words
the one and the other
always fascinating
and I
bewildered by
the literalism in figurative language
tested
an egg on a sidewalk
on a day
when someone said it was hot
enough to
fry an egg on a sidewalk
the sidewalk globbed
and when my sister said
she and a friend had painted the whole town red
I found not one dab of paint
the disappointment did not dissuade me
I still believed
in poetry
the pictures in words
and the persistent possibility
of making the one from the other
but could never avoid
the spellbound cracks on sidewalks
confused white lies
and blackmail
green thumbs
and red letter days
and the ambiguous dread
in double negative interrogation
("Did you not understand what you did was wrong?")
after I had played hookey
in grade one
and invented a story
about two friends named Somebody and Nobody
which satisfied my whims
(Somebody had a birthday party and Nobody came)
of ambiguity
and paradox
and thus by turns
turned
words
into

pictures
turned
into
words
by
way
of
a
biographical
self
portrait

Ike Mills' Finishing School

As fresh manure draws flies, Ike's place drew kids
who, after four, biked by to roll in it:
horse sweat, caked collars, whiskey breath,
his growled threats to upend you
into the packing crate, leaning on the tin siding wall,
heaped-up with soiled hay, urine-mud, horseballs,
vomit, eggshells, empties, parts of lives.
Scare-talk nine times out of ten,
kindled anticipation on a fire of fear;
the tenth—when Ike had drunk himself cranky,
turned a touch cantankerous—
he'd lift a kid up by the heels, raise the lid, drop him in.
While the kid gaped in bewilderment that bluff turned real,
his gruffness would command him to skedaddle home;
"Tell your ma you need a bath, you stinky little bastard!"

Dark stable: sunlight sears a white brilliant sword between the slats,
piercing macules in sullen air.
Cats' eyes glow greenly here, for where there's grain there're mice;
Ike forked a mouse family once into a wheel-barrow,
small pink bodies, slight, small screaming,
scooped them into the bin of fouled hay,
then threw a cat in to end their misery.

Like a tossed aside scatter rug, Ike's remaining dog,
half hound-of-Hell, half Lab, half-starved, half-cur,
growling gutturals in dreams of racing over snow,
its legs jerk out and jump,
snapping in his traces on a crusty lake.
Ike in glory gleaming, mutters "Sic'em!"
to see us start; in raucous laughter,
head a-wobble like a raven's,
taking pleasure in the fears of children.

House sparrows contend for oats in khaki dung;
horses' tails thrash flies away;
we pull a hose across the lot
to fill the lengthwise-sawed hot water tank,
water trough beside the foxtails.
Ike persuades us it's a task for yeomen earning knighthood
an ocean farther, a thousand years remote
from ballads of lingering love and lonely horsemen.

We learned to spit there—both distance and control—
shovel horseshit, soap saddles, sweep dust
around the concrete floor of his cave-like shed
where a cowboy with a lantern-jaw rocks on a kitchen chair,
dime-storing a roll-yer-own on a web of spittle,
peering from beneath a black ten-gallon Stetson,
watching us do the chores he promised Ike he'd do
when Ike ambled down the alley to the Eddy
to quaff a dozen beers before the bar closed at suppertime.

In June long days when the sandy soil of the yard withers,
Ike or Lantern-Jaw hoses the lot down,
sprays the horses reined to the rail to cool them off
where they shift feet, awaiting dudes,
sprays a kid as easily.

Ike's horses know where to go, how far, how fast, when to turn;
no wheedle, whip, or kick or coax will move them further.
They know their gait, their pace, turn
before a rein can gee or haw them,
know how far an hour will take them
before they trot an hour back,
knowing tourists usually hire a horse two hours.

A young woman in blue jeans, an emerald satin shirt
with bright black piping, hangs around the stable,
"Charmayne" on one breast pocket,
"Yippee!" in white cotton cable on the other.
A blush of lust arousing ten-year olds' imaginations,
twelve-year olds' anticipations,
glimpsed breast flesh bulging from bra cups,
pressing up and in and out,
pretending to understand the japes Lantern-Jaw alludes to:
"Mare's been rid hard—put away wet!"

She understands buttons the way Ike knows kids:
how close to keep them to the heart, how far to let one go,
when to loosen one a moment to see what happens.
British Empire pink, her flesh puckers where she's cinched,
pressing a satin frontier of French Imperial green.

In the kitchen, at the oilclothed table, sits Alma Mills.
Into a bugle glass Ike snitched from the beer parlour
pours the butt of a beer,
lights a cork-tipped Black Cat from the ember of the last,
wondering whether eggs and beans will do for supper,
if he'll be home for supper sober,
while kids clamber over the chuckwagon,
its conestoga bonnet top pretending
western movies, a ring of covered wagons, Apache raids
beneath the fading sign:
"Ike Mills' Riding School—Horses for Hire
"Outfitted Trips Available by Arrangement."

Hot still air of late afternoon;
in shrieks and giggling, the afternoon's recessional,
Lantern-Jaw tail-ties sixteen horses in a line,
saddles four, and four kids ride bareback.
Dust, whinnying, shod hooves clattering on asphalt,
golden sun, wind rustling the leaves of the great poplar
in George Moore's yard next door,
and Lantern-Jaw driving an aged pickup.

Dust-devil blurring barn-red warehouse,
rain pocking horseshoe prints in dust,
a tawny cat flees.

A half-hour later Lantern-Jaw drives into the yard,
the promise of a woman leaning on his shoulder,
the truck box unloads its kids who disperse on bikes,
departing the afternoon,
lessons of Ike's Finishing School for Boys.
Lantern-Jaw steers the emerald satin Seven Years' War
through the barn-style doors toward the weary Winnipeg couch.

Alma sees them disappear from view,
wondering if he closed the doors.
She eats little, but Alma is hungry;
knows surely as she makes a sandwich,
Ike'll expect her to eat when he comes in—when he comes in.
Low clouds crawl above the spruce trees
on the lower mountain slopes.
The rain keeps falling, falling.
More green the trees now for the dust the rain has washed away;
in failing dusk the green intensifies
beneath blue-grey clouds.
Blackness of shadows emerges from the velvet green,
an almost-silence takes the night
except for eaves' drips and the waterspout.

A bawling howl at midnight:
from the numbness settled into her
Alma shakes her head,
slowly moves toward the door.
The rain is falling still.
Misty softness of the streetlight glow
envelops him: standing naked in the rain,
his arms and hands outstretched,
head bent to the night, his paunch lopped down,
in storm and darkness baying in a language only he can understand
to darkness and the dog, to bats and owls, to rain and thunder,

seeming what he hasn't seemed in years,
naked and innocent, mud on his hands, blood on his knees
where he has stumbled, fallen, crawled,
standing to let the June rain cleanse him.

INVENTING STYLES

FALLING *in* LOVE

Falling in love with what he'd written,
taking note of skill and craft,
either he was daft or smitten,
confused the ardor and, no doubt,
what she thought he wrote about.

He fell in love with what he'd written,
believing nominally it concerned
the woman it seemed to be about,
and hence by typical delusion
fell zatch over guggle into confusion,

falling in love with whom he'd written,
believing her to be the poem,
bedded her inside the home
he'd made of words, and on the shelf
neatly placed her in himself.

Alma Ata

A great shell cast upon the beach the desert is
against the sheer rampart of the dragon range, Tien Shan,
Alma Ata, Father of Apples, Kazakhstan, the northern Turkomans,
sits on the fan that is the shell
where we sit in the plane, upon the plain the desert is
and wait for Popov's argument to end.

Soviet bureaucracy, so much for it, has oversold the seats
and seatless standing Popov will not leave the plane.

Dragons dance cadenzas in the heat,
the Tien Shan captured dragons,
shimmering ribbons in the tatters of the scrubbrush
and ripples of the Turkoman past flap in on us:
our plane will not depart till Popov's disputation's settled.
The voices rise in rocketry, exploding star-wheels in the sky,
Chinese candles, buzz bombs, flares, and flaring tempers
raise the passenger compartment's temperature
as everybody's temper flares.
Why not just pop Popov off the plane?

The air crew leaves the cabin, strolls down the aisle,
embarrassment in their smiles at us
encouraging us to understand?

And Popov's anger continues to crescendo.

Irina, Intourist escort excellente, chatters with a stew
who grants permission for us to leave the swelter of the plane
the smelter of the passions.

Among the dragons on the tarmac
in the shadow of the wing we stand and gossip:
<<I thought they'd simply force him out and have him walk the plank.>>
<<Is he a party member then, Irina?>>
<<Is that how he can get away with this?>>
She will not answer.
<<How long has he been waiting?>>
<<How often does this happen?>>

It's cooler in the desert on the asphalt than in the plane.
Some other passengers disembark.
Heat haze hides the mountains.
Only Popov and the stewardess are on the plane.

A fuel line boas through the grass and beneath the belly of the plane.
Talking and laughing among themselves,
several passengers are sitting on it,
gesticulating, distending lower lips in their profound disdain
of comrade Popov who would make such a scene
and do it too in front of tourists
and sharing cigarettes among themselves and lighting them.

We point out the open flames, the cigarettes, the casual
tossed-to-the-winds caution of the smoking comrades
to the air crew
who smile comprehendingly
and thank us for pointing out the danger
and saunter several hundred yards away to the dry grass at the runway's edge.

I wish I could report the conflagration in the plane
became the flame of dragons' nostrils spewing forth
into the shimmering atmospheres
of Alma Ata, consuming Popov in his fury,
but nothing seems to happen here in Alma Ata
beneath the dragons of the border
and the great ribbed hills,
the alluvial fan.

I wish I could report I understood what happened,
but excellente escort Intourist Irina did not know
or would not tell.

We were given the sign to reboard the plane
and Popov smiling had a seat
and no one was left behind

nor did the smokers set the plane afire.

Eyes' Size

If our eyes
were of a size
as proportionate to
our size
as a peregrine's eyes
are to its size
our eyes
would be the size
of softballs

(<<found>> in *The Peregrine,* by R.H. Baker)

LARIX LYALLII   *for Jean Finley*

Its adaptations sequester it in the narrow zone,
    a lonely last high place for trees
    where persistence and resilience
    measure survival, grudge, and fitness on
    bare rock, in thin soil, its competence
    unquestioned (it has no competition);
    it does not scrabble on its knees,
    like krummholz firs, against dessication
but angulates recalcitrant in black Sunday best
    nine months, or, like tormented cocktail
        ladies in grey chiffon
stretches arms in gloves for its expression.

Its young needles may be used for a kind of soup.
    It has <<about nine relatives,>> we read,
    and two in Canada, the Western Larch
and Tamarack, deciduous conifers, which share shape
    with dead spruce at the swamp march
    and on bog edge, like misanthropes,
    their dying unattended, unwept,
    varying true to genotype,
grey ministers in a grove of younger trees,
    bible-black, covering their limbs
        with snow and hope.
The bare branch skeleton is an archetype.

From its fingers' warts in sprays, soft like
     small fountains or needle-ice needles
     of a softness akin to kittens' whiskers
leaves unfurl like chenille. We could make the mistake,
     unless we employed our fingers,
     of thinking them the hard spike
     of fir or pine, the rapiers
     willows bespeak,
but lo, they relent, submitting to late snowfalls
     of the wet June heaviest sort
        and do not break
but, reverberant, apparently kick back.

Their needles are hung so as to filter not obscure
     the sunlight, a green lace mantilla
     worn exotically among anemones
and dogtooth violets, moss campions that persevere
     the wind and sleet, friends in enemies,
     pikas, marmots, ptarmigans that endure
     among lichens the dappling felicities
     that dress the fellfield in grey-green and ochre
making of the alpine slopes a gaiety
     the forty frost-free days, if that,
        before the sere
winds strip needles and petals without care.

This rarest seen of trees in grey bark garbed
     in the Rockies no norther than Hector Lake
     persists; economically of aesthetic purpose only;
was named by David Lyall, a surveyor of the border
     who found it near the home of conies

making hay on rocks beside it undisturbed.
In September, a week before the aspens shake
their gold, sun's equinoctial orb
and deep frost turn the pale and wanly
green needles an instant gold,
a gold in blue enrobed,
flung for a day; and in a day they're drab.

DIDACTYLLIC

Bugaboo, Cariboo:
Dryas drummondii
nods in the breeze like the
Black-headed Fleabane

known as *Erigeron
melanocephalus,*
snug in its jacket in
snow and in rain.

technopaegnia

Poem in form of labyrinth

the rules of the game stipulate you may only pass   through where you have not yet passed previously

mind   hero
maze   only a topological idiot begins at the middle but there he would start at the minotaur   king
ways   mirrored   seek
wind   clearest   supercalifragilisticexpialidocious   the initiation into absolute realities   lost
into   drear   and   winding   can   tricks   mute
form   muddy   always   miscomprehensions   internal   despair   many   win   myriad   trials   awry
amid   murky   as   labyrinthine   tortures   ways   the   errors   misery   path
word   foggy   situational   inclinations   grace counterproductivity   big   abound   memory   gone
play   angry   if   stress   but   as   one   misted   spaces   agee
with   alone   it   blackens   now   honorificibilitudinitatibus   at   but   in the   gloomy   dire
wise   as   be   for   led   out   from   an   not   silent   abject   sand
wits   misapprehensive   any   low   way   sesquepedalian   what   oh   tie   enigma   terror   lead
also   all   dim   for   him   septuagenarian   will   we   the   around   losing   away
amusements   yet   for   way   you   for   transmogrifies   be   do   end   puzzle   string   from
atrocities   who   any   far   who   web   fear   not   so   bend   middle   wall
perturbing   may   shy   out   did   and   into   o   for   of   in inoperative mischief   catacombs
involution   bay   sly   bet   net   bull   a   him   no   a   nearer
disturbing   buy   particularities   her   minotaur   but   inconsequanciality often   page   danger
intimation   cry   perhaps   let   id   for   as   nor   lame   darker
omnivorous   out   wayward   Ariadne's magic thread   the   if   reappearances   one   weak   vaster
dismayings   woe   mishaps   one   it   so   how   nor   face   deeper
amazements   all   apprenticeship for the neophytes   who   be   be   if   all   two   is   always
heed   day   being   to   can   in   it   it   can   but   by   confused
need   lamenting   paths   an amplification of   be   win   an   be   pan   ten   us   dismayed
want   gnashings   found   fun   dry   in   his   ambidextrous   out   for   as   diffused
loss   tormented   along   yet   Theseus   wry   it   way   tauromachian   ill   the   we   huddle
fail   innerness   route   not   old   as   out   yet   man   hide   wonder
fall   hint   angle   new   misanthropist   in   ambivalently in the last   who   bump   wander
lame   that   mythifying   but   or   in   an   eschatological   had   hunt   pander
lose   near   miraculous   old   by   can   it   incorrigible   Shakespeherian   set   miss   simper
limb   here   intramural   age   an   one   entrancement   venerabilities   out   muse   dodder
slip   were   meddlement   can   id   outsmart   with no exit   overwhelmingly   the   fade   weep
slop   some   try   be   Daedalus   of   map   bended   sift
mere   gravel   blind blunderers   on   antidisestablishmentarianist   overambitiously   waning   flop
atom   an   architectonic   to   as   away
floccipaucinihilipilifications   anomic   bewilderments   misunderstand   phantasmagoria   if   slip
find   vagary   underhandedly   mystery   in   hope
flay   the loss of the spirit as an illusion in the act of creation   history   honeycomb   near
slay   concealedly   ends
or like its maker and his son make wings of feathers with wax and fly toward the sun and escape thus

poems for children

Dinosaurs Mean So Much *to* Morris

Dinosaurs mean so much to Morris
he reads about them every day.
He plans to raise a brontosaurus.

The Badlands are beckoning Morris and Horace
to capture a baby one there, if they may—
dinosaurs mean so much to Morris.

When they find one, they'll name him "Boris."
"They're nice," says Morris. He knows they're grey.
He plans to raise a brontosaurus.

"Too big," Mommy argues. "Boris will floor us!"
"Boris," says Morris, "won't be in the way."
Dinosaurs mean so much to Morris.

"Boris," says Morris, "will really adore us;
they're clean and they're quiet. They like to play."
He plans to raise a brontosaurus.

Morris and Horace, their voices in chorus,
say "Boris is sweet!" That's what <u>they</u> say!
Dinosaurs mean so much to Morris
he plans to raise a brontosaurus.

THE PLACE WHERE *the* LOST THINGS GO

When we were children
passing through spring,
wondering what happened to snow,
we should have known
the wind had blown
all to the place where the lost things go

Right hand mittens,
tortoiseshell kittens,
the minute hand from the broken clock,
the second book of *Lord of the Rings,*
Mother's copy of *Captain and Kings,*
Daddy's diamond left foot sock;
paper, tracing;
gum, erasing;
the whatzit used for puffing chalk on hems,
the credit card for Texaco,
the family's slides of Mexico;
the vase's frog for holding flower stems.

If you should go there,
you'll know it at once:
it's the place where the lost things go;
they're piled in heaps
and jumbled confusion
and buried in last year's snow.

My brother says I lost the twelfth red checker.
He lost the ladder for the double-decker
bunkbed, and from the deck of cards he lost the King of Hearts,

the Christmas window spraycan snow,
the minerals to make the flowers grow,
and Daddy's box of they'll-come-in-useful-someday parts;
nor can he find his hockey stick,
his hockey cards, his guitar pick
or any time to ever play with me,
the helicopter model that he built when he was ten,
the address of the girl he'll never find again,
and the shells he collected by the sea.

People are wandering
hither and yon
in the place where the lost things go,
searching in vain
for all the lost things
carried where guesses go.

My sister's lost her diary key,
with it her sense of mystery
she strived for months to find;
the glue to fix her false eyelashes,
two (or more) or her teenage mashes;
I've even heard her say she's lost her mind.
In the book she's reading she's lost her place,
a thing she will not name, but I know it's made of lace;
she cannot keep a secret for a week;
a string of Mother's imitation pearls,
and an earring, one of Shirl's;
and more than once her voice—which really made her meek,
Hidden in bushes,
shrubs, and by rushes,
carried by time and the river's flow;
in closets and batches,

in tumult and snatches:
this is the place where the lost things go.

Mother says she lost her heart
to Daddy, and her appetite for eating à la carte;
in Mexico a leather sandal
and one part of a paisley
measly
slightly freeform bikini, causing just a little scandal;
she believes at times her sanity,
the mirror from her vanity,
and she also lost her maiden name;
also her virginity, verily
but merrily;
and just two nights ago at bridge she lost the game.

Harsh winds have taken
the forgotten, forsaken
things to the place where the lost things go;
and they will never
return, not ever:
just like the past and the snow.

Daddy says he loses bets;
in Saskatchewan his fishing nets.
Last Sunday on a drive he lost the way—
he lost the map
and in a flap
he could not find the proper thing to say.
He's lost his delusions,
his boyhood illusions,
and the urge to mow the lawn;
nor can he find a cufflink

that was here just an eyeblink
ago, or tell where the years have gone.

Time and the gremlins
have borne them away,
further than we'll ever know,
but they're just around corners
off in a drift
to the place where the lost things go.

INVENTING *the* CANADIAN ROCKIES

The Agony *of* Mrs. Stone

Part I

1: Sunday, July 17, 1921

A statement isolated
between a question it poses
a question unanswered—

how she endured seven days
on the mountain

Her husband fell
from the summit of Eon
into death's isolation

"I can see nothing higher"
he had shouted
from the mountain's height
then fell

The rope

She sees him falling past her
waits for
braces for his weight

sees him fall

The body falls from ledge to ledge
dropping from sight in slowest motion
until it seems "it must have gone . . .
to the bottom of the mountain side . . ."

Stillness and isolation

Between the heavens and the earth
sun sets on the first day

2: Monday, July 18, 1921

Cautiously
she coils the rope
in the dawn

Dawn
clinging the summit
has not declined to the valley

No warmth of red glows in the cloudless dawn
Hot and pale it will be

Never so alone

Silver water trickles on a far mountain's face
Black forest waking beneath grey mountains

Descent alone

He had unroped
He had seen nothing higher
His ice axe held in his hand as he fell

Thirsty

She is very thirsty

Snow lies below on the mountain's steep south slope

Slight warmth in the sun

Stares into the chimney's gape

up which he'd scrambled

She had never climbed alone

By sunset of her first long day
she made her way by crumbling rock
to a ledge above the lower ledges

Climbing down is moving on a point
letting the mountain ascend
How strange
not to have noticed it

Delayed in searching for his body
she hoped might still have life
she bivouaced above the lower ledges
when darkness came

3: Tuesday, July 19, 1921

Must have slept
she could not remember sleeping
She had no dreams

Her elbows jostle her ribs
She distends a yawn to cease her teeth's chattering

Hears, she thinks, water trickling

On the infirm rock in the warming day
descends

They expected us yesterday
When we're not back today, they'll come looking
I'll meet them

By a rock tower she mistakes their route
taking a lower ledge narrowing to sheer cliff
retraces her steps ascending
sees a scree slope
beneath a chimney
seemingly descending
to the trees

By the ledge below

It is safe
leads a hundred feet to the slope
then the scree to the trees and camp

Warm again, her thirst slaked

Winds herself into the rope
turns her face to the wall
tests a rock; it is solid
fixes the rope
leans back
out down into the chimney

The ledge nears
The rope shortens
She is at the end of it
The ledge so close
She dangles at the rope's end
then drops the last ten feet

The rope swings above her
No need of it
She walks the ledge
feels its broad, level assurance
relieved to walk on its flat

The ledge narrows

A rock rattles loose and chatters away

She holds to the wall

The ledge is narrow now, too narrow

The scree slope seems so near

She edges her way back
explores the other end of the ledge

Thirsty

The ledge is closed

Nor up, nor down, nor off

The rope swinging above her
She cannot reach it
Tries to build a ramp of rocks but they are scant
She cannot reach it
The scree slope is near but she lacks the skill, the strength
lacks the rope

She takes her handkerchief from her pocket

Cannot cry

In a cleft a droplet of water

Jams the cotton into the crack
watches the handkerchief darken with the stain of damp

Today they are expected back

She winds her watch
times the hours it takes for her hanky to dampen for one sweet quench

Curls her head between her knees
sleeps
Easier to sleep in the sun
stay awake the night

4: Wednesday, July 20, 1921

Today they will come
Anticipated yesterday at the latest
failing to arrive
we'll . . . I'll be looked for today
Today they'll send someone

Four hours for the drops to drench the hanky
three more at the most

Her stomach knots

Thinks about him rarely
thinks about water

their arrival
remembers the moss
how she put stale lips to it
could not draw its water out

Takes the cap from her watch
presses it into the moss
all her strength

It fills
The pressed moss yields its water
She drinks the capful, tries again
Only a few more drops

Soon they will be coming
Her throat must be wet enough to shout
Must not be greedy and force the moss dry

Bleak bands of cloud turn apricot, crimson, purple-black
as the light dies

5: Thursday, July 21, 1921

They made their way to the mountain yesterday
arrived at dark
They are up at the first light
beginning the search

She hears them moving in the darkness
tries to shout
but her dry throat
rattles a raven's croak
and she wakes
to the dark chill
can neither sleep nor stay awake

The sky lightens

She sees dawn inch down the slope
sees a flood of light
hears water fall to far away Gloria

In the sun's warmth she uncurls and lies in it

She must get up. She must walk. She must if . . .

She has strength; keep her muscles moving
make the rescue easier when
if they come

be ready to help

when they come

listen

The shade comes

The seeping water does not suffice

They do not come

They came
she thinks

came while she slept
she had not heard them

6: Friday, July 22, 1921

The days become nights
The ledge becomes a wall
that she is falling from
the nights days
and waiting action

She can not stay awake
and stays awake
hears voices always

A spider wobbles over pebbles
spins a web of gossamer
between two rocks
Waits for flies to become trapped

They had come
found nothing

looked
shouted
and she had thought them dream

Why do they not come?

A mountain is too huge

She hears the cries of birds
The forest is not so far below that birds are alien

Puffed eyes, burnt arms, stiff and thickening fingers

No longer thinks about thinking
his death

Thinks about the water bottle in his pack

Things become more important than thoughts

Hears voices
a calling
hears a ringing
raises her head, leaning it drowsily listening

Hears nothing

Waste no hopes and thoughts on fantasies

Water and peace
the clear reflection in the still lake

Her lips drink the damp now before her mouth

Her pores call out
Tries with numb fingers to scrape the cheating dust from her lips

Her pores call out

Drop by drop falling away from her

She would have a storm
snow and ice for their water
fountains to walk among
soft lush wet grass
tears
breakers
the pockmarks of water drops in dust

the shrivelling

The rope hangs above her

She lies on her back
stares at it

Night falls

7: Saturday, July 23, 1921

The spider caught and killed a fly
encasing it in silk

Go away, death, this ledge is too narrow

I knew you would come
You won't deceive me easily

or are you here to give me consolation?

Despair came with you

words wheeling
trying to keep in motion
the sphere of silence you'd impose

The exhilerating dizziness

We become smaller

a sense of looking up

mountain's visitors

gradually unfolding

Damn you, let me sleep

distended veins in the cold hands

Now my finger traces in the air as on a map the route

"nothing higher . . ."

stillness and isolation

earth, air, fire

where's water?

essentials

Deepset eyes glowing red with blood

Silence frames

permanence in ice

The marmots whistle on the scree below

If marmots whistle, there's reason for alarm

"Nothing higher . . ."

Nothing

8: Sunday, July 24, 1921

Slowly the light blurs her dry eyes in smears

She does not know time

Her swelled tongue
her scratched fingers do not heal

A scrabble of pebbles falls near her
She dares not move
Must pull herself to the edge to peer

She waits for the quilt of darkness

Death descends
not like the hawk or eagle plunging
but crawling upon her gently like the spider

The frail filament holding her will sever

She will lose her weight and his
like a loose web float on the rising air
swoop, waft, plume, and plummet

It flares, the candle sputters
the phoenix in the flame rises
the maples of autumn burning brightest

The white light on the gray rock blanches its features

They came and have gone

The light is darkness
and hope is despair

The mountain is a pit she must climb up from

Ecstasy a furrow

A stain upon the rock
my substance is my spirit

Soft voices at a garden party
Ice is clinking in the lemonade

It's so hot in Indiana in July
we should be in the mountains
Ah, our happy home, the tabernacled sky
umbrellas, parasols, clouds
a breeze from the river cools

Which day is it how long has it been celebrate the living

Serene here in the garden until it happens
I wish the autos didn't backfire so, scares the horses
why must the screen door slam
cannon at dusk   the lowering flag   seems   so beautiful
against the sky   it's fading

They've gone   against the sky

She shouts
hears a shout, a shot, echoing and subsiding
draws from the cleft the hanky
sucks it

Shouts again
hears a shout, shot, echoing and subsiding

Out of the dusk
from above
on a rope
in the long dusk of summer
Rudolf
descending

"Rudolf," she whispers, "I knew you would come . . ."

Then she sleeps

Part II

Margaret Stone is the questions she has become

Photographs of her in albums almost reveal a face
shadowed as it is by wide-brimmed hats
underexposed, at distances too great for detail
in darkness against white snow, in profile against the sky

In the shadow of her husband's death
and in the shadow of her long days and nights
she persists in the meagre knowledge
we have of her
endures perennially the ledge she endured a week
the ledge she still endures in memory
collapsing on Eon's rotten rock
an echelon of questions

Still night stars' slow rotating
space, night, days, ledge, life—
the rope in the chimney above the bleak, grey rock to the mountain's top
and the rope in the chimney above the ledge of her endurance
curl into question marks
to questions that cannot be answered—

When you pieced your shattering together
what pieces where you missing?

What was your face before time chiselled it?
Always in shadow?

Beyond the smoke and in the shade
Mount Eon in the backdrop
reclining almost visible
Margaret Stone in the last photograph taken by her husband

She persisted
She endured these things:
    reduction
    solitude
    pain
    thirst
    cold
    hunger
    loneliness
    struggle
    futility
    despair
    time
    waiting
    fear
    panic
    survival
    duration
    fantasy
    seven days
time enough to make a world
lose a mind
she held

The statement is suspended above a cleft:
why was her wait so long?

In 1921 the Assiniboine region was wild. From Magog, Gog, by Wonder Pass to Marvel Lake, by Gloria and Terrapin to Marvel Pass and Eon's base there was no trail.

A photo taken the year before by Dr. Stone reveals the panoramic sweep of Mounts Gloria, Eon, Aye, a picture lingered over for a year in Lafayette, placed in the mosaic by Mrs. Stone.

Dr. and Mrs. Stone, "anxious to crown a big one," sought the mystery and the reward, but sought them cautiously. In yielding to the mountain, they found, leaving unanswered, the questions they have become: Dr. Stone, an Icarus falling, falling from peak, and Margaret Stone a Tantalus in thirst, Prometheus below an eagle-circled sky.

Times burns their personalities away. Pieced photos show the mountain and their route from Marvel Pass.

Why was her agony so long?

The Stones were expected back at the summer climbing camp, the Jubilee Camp of the Alpine Club at Assiniboine, a day after their accident occurred.

The first evening and night that Mrs. Stone spent below the summit, the Stones were supposed to be descending.

Her first full day, when she descended to the ledges, they were to be returning.

Her second day, the entrapment, the people in the camp spent in darkening doubt about their safety.

The third day a party made its way to Marvel Pass and found the Stones' camp. A full reconnaissance was made the fourth day, two days after the Stones were supposed to have returned. Help was sent for in Banff, but Mount Assiniboine is a full day's travel from the town.

The fifth day, Bill Peyto, packer, and Rudolf Aemmer, the Swiss guide, made the forty-five miles to Assiniboine in one day. The sixth day Peyto and Aemmer moved to Marvel Pass.

The seventh day was spent in the search. "It was growing late, when they were startled by hearing a call from a point to the westward."

Help could have come sooner had it come directly from Assiniboine, but no one in the camp believed he had the competence to effect a rescue.

"They discovered Mrs. Stone on a ledge almost a quarter of a mile away and 300 feet below them."

The final photo in the albums is of the summit cairn erected by the men who brought back the body of Winthrop Stone, and noted by her pen's white ink on the black paper.

Part III

The essentials: earth, air, fire
The mountains strip the rest away and leave
bare rock in wind and sun

The blood of lichens, the green of trees
the mountains leave behind

They move in titans' time
slow
imperceptibly altering from age to age
apart from life
void of life
a taunt of time

The epilogue tells less

In late September, 1975, I wrote Purdue
where Winthrop Stone was President
inquiring if it were known
what had become of Mrs. Stone
learned she had moved from Lafayette in 1923
or so
It was not known where she had gone

The legend of the ledge persists

In late November, '75, on an off chance
I mentioned the mystery to Evelyn Moorhouse
who asked
if the Stones were members of the Alpine Club

Rotting layer cakes
they look like Parthenons or Roman temples
and fall apart by a hand's tug or a stiff wind

Club records indicate in 1923 that Mrs. Stone
life member
moved to Sheffield in the Berkshires
there lived till 1967 or thereabouts
the records for that year say "address unknown"
and then her name disappears from the rolls

Lakes below glimmer, gathering indigo

I wrote the town clerk, Sheffield, heard no more

Too close, you sidle too near

In May of '76, a day low hung with clouds
and snow upon the summits of the rounded mountains
where Melville first met Hawthorne
by Stockbridge where Norman Rockwell lives
Walt Kelly lived
and Alice's Restaurant closed down that month
where Daniel Chester French had his studio
south of Tanglewood and Lenox
by Great Barrington and Sheffield Plain
we proceeded to Shelfield
a small, secluded Berkshires town

Minnie Markham, town clerk, born in Sheffield, 1926
had never heard of Mrs. Stone

Enthralled by the story

The legend of the ledge persists

Warren Wesley, postmaster of Sheffield since the war
had never heard of Mrs. Stone

The legend of the ledge persists

Wisps of cloud move about the mountain's slopes

Storms pass, the mountain wears away
Ice forms on the summit about the cairn topped by his axe
erected to his memory

The ledge is silent

Unseen since and still
the ledge is silent

July 27, 1976
September 8, 1976
March 10, 1977

HOMAGE, HENRY KELSEY
Part ye First

List

The material relating to Henry Kelsey is so meagre that even the most commonplace fragments may be worthy of record. —ARTHUR G. DOUGHTY AND CHESTER MARTIN, INTRODUCTION, *The Kelsey Papers*, XXIV

                    Ungava
              not the land Ungava
        beyond horizon where man feels home
                      but
                    ungava
                in the eye's lee
                   until a

moment grasps man   by his imagination
stretching in yearning   relaxing his thoughts

                    Ungava
              is sallied forth from
           England is an ungava

and in the reek of spring's melting
          in summer's florescence
          in patch-spotted swathing
          in maturing
here is not a land beyond the eye or memory
          in winter's dim and still
          beyond vision's rim
but   here

                      I

                     am
                   Ungava
           quickened by paddle's brush
                gliding canoe
        through silent lake and riverrush

If this wont do farewell to all as I may say
And for my living i'll seek some other way

Speaking to himself, he speaks to us

In sixteen hundred & ninety'th year
I set forth as plainly may appear
through Gods assistance for to understand
The natives language & to see their land
And for my masters interest I did soon
Sett from ye house ye twealth of June

out of isolation

Then up ye River I with heavy heart
Did take my way & from all English part
To live amongst ye Natives of this place
If god permits me for one two years space

Seekwan
and the trumpeter swan returns
the long-beaked whimbrel shores to summerhome
curlews whisper in the lengthening dusk and dawn of
spring
as seekwan is noise again
nostrils twitching odours from the snow's melt
the sun felt is seekwan
beneath the daily climbing sun
seek wandering
eyes rise
to the blunt horizon
it is

spring rivulets creeks flooding anew rivers flowing
forcing their ice to pack, crush, melt, overflow,
rumbling the heart stirring in the bosque of
                    seek wondering
spring in the spring of birds and their song returning
buds, birds, cubs, calves, fawns and dawns warm
and incredible in the sparkle, ooze and hues of green,
seeping, washing waters and the rotting mosses' reek
                    seek wander
            and be born again beyond
        the sun setting lustwandering
                no time for rest
stir, step, stride, walk, wander, follow, pursue,
                sequent seekwan

Between the tangent drawn aslant the dream's nivation
of sense: the way things seem: locus of history about
                a centre
        a vision forming landscape
            a manner of seeing
        in the current of circumstance
    by the south branch of the middle road

From ye house six hundred miles southwest
Through Rivers wch run strong with falls
thirty three Carriages five lakes in all

(by the Knee, Oxford, Walker, Cross, and Moose)

to travel and to penetrate into the country
of the Assinae Poets, with the Captain of that Nation
to call, encourage, and invite the remoter Indians
to a trade with us

the Echimamish
flows both ways

West to the Nelson   East to the Hayes
in time
dawnhunter in barrens
hunter of mastadon, mammoth
fear of the soft-stepping tiger
the giant bear lording his domain
at glaciers' toe

Upon
the debacle in spring
frazil surfacing in autumn's decline
in the rivers' sinews beneath the sun-dogged sky

Kelsey stands

Hail, Kelsey, come: the land is not barren,
land of little sticks, caribou lichen, musketers only;
come to the land: the land is not barren,
the land that is mused, is browsed, is fused
by mooseways over, among, between, and through
the muskrat-slickened banks of oozing mud,
its list aboil, aswarm with mosquitoes,
the must of melting and dispersing such a wonder
of flying, biting, cloud turmoiling things;
come to the land: the land is not barren;
the glaciers' scores on the rusty rock reveal
that life withdrew but has returned;
come, Kelsey, come to the land.

The Inland Country of Good report hath been
By Indians but by English yet not seen
Therefore I on my Journey did not stay
But making all ye hast I could upon our way
Gott on ye borders of y^e stone Indian Country
I took possession on y^e tenth Instant July
And for my masters I speaking for y^m all
This neck of land I deerings point did call

Name, namer, new master now
with fame ill-fit on Rupert's Land
trading across three centuries

> *for the use and benefitt of the Govr*
> *and $Comp^y$ of adventurers of England*
> *trading into Hudsons Bay and their Successors*

ourselves as well, who cannot be so easily assured,

> *Thou dost not know the hardships I endur'd*
> *In this same desert where Ever y^t I have been*

Just   In the web and texture of the land
is woven more than we can understand

> *Nor wilt thou me believe without y^t thou had seen*
> *The Emynent Dangers that did often me attend*

It does not begin nor end, hence we converse:
hunger, the stomach shrinking, the masked rocks of rapids,
the abuse of anger, the flare of feelings amid fear
and companions' enemies, canoes overturning, fire,
starvation peering through the lankness of the clouds,

fear of murder in the insolence of midnight,
being lost in uncharted woods in winter
where rivers fall away to darkness,
gestures of friendship taken as defiance,
unfamiliar beasts, unknown customs, the undiscovered hemlocks,
unease, disease, and always the threat
the land's maw will swallow a man
nor leave a trace of him on swamp or grassland,
in trees or in the woodland meadow,
deceiving man who thinks he knows himself

Language falls behind in the rivers' newness,
rumoured to run red as murderous blood in summer's flood,
of flesh-smooth land as soft as youth,
as old as archaic stone the glacier bared to sun.

> *But still I was resolved this same Country for to see*
> *Although through many dangers I did pass*
> *Hoped still to undergo y^m at the Last*

It flows both ways

Calving glacial ice,
the blue-green dragon
meets in gravel
lichens breaking the greyness in golden rust,
and south, as the ice-chilled wind warmed,
came soft-spring-green grass
rooting in the till and rotting, forming soil
for hunter to walk upon softly, silently
as great cats walk.

> The woods creep north to where they grow no higher
> and who would live there hunts without hiding.

Rivers meander
grey in the misted morning: thick daybreak

    Silence is born of the marriage of deep wonder and winter

Morning song of meadowlark
rejoicing from wild rice stalks

    Sky blueness blunts the horizon

Stillness
the centre of wonder

Is
Ungava
obscured within the mind
beyond a loon-called loneliness?

The fog clings to the slow waters

It is time to shuck the hides, tighten muscles,
slide the canoes from the slick banks into the musty air,
glide on the ripples, seek the misted sun through oblique shadows

seek the river

in the muskrat country
between the tracks
upon a pan of snow

seek Miss-Top-Ashish
Little Giant
Henry Kelsey

The land you saw we cannot begin to see
'til what you see reveals the world,
and we have just begun to be aware of an Ungava
about to brim up in our eyes and solitudes

in the wildlands and in your Ungava yet

we see you

now
standing in the
world alone
you made

Part ye Second

Etomomi

. . . he had been so near to ye sun at ye going down
y^t he could take hold of it when it Cut ye Horrizon—THE KELSEY PAPERS, 23

Once we know where once he was,
    we cannot tell when he was there;
whither once he went we know,
    we cannot tell when he was thither.

Where	Then
and when	and there
at the mind's edge	it is always dark
at its edges	I squint
beyond me	my shadow
is no substance	dissipates
unstriking light	in darkness
at the warmth's edge	I turn my back
where the	trees glimmer
last shadow	engulfed in shadow
standing	peering into darkness
I fancy	I see
I see movement	I hope
I hesitate	my eyes darting
in the gloom	I thought it black
now it's night	bleak
darkness	mute
more than mute	carbon silence
absorbent	unrelinquishing
adumbrated	deep
directionless	bearingless

I could turn	back to blackness
gaze into the fire	my hands bask in
its pale phantoms	cold comfort
attract	in the chill
the edges	fade
the dark's ways	into luke-dim
unending	silence

But still I lived in hopes y^t once it would amend
And makes me free from Hunger & from Cold
Likewise many other things wch I cannot here unfold

knowing	which way they'd gone
I'd not be lost	in terror
not knowing	if their way is
doubting	alert to absence
in skepticism	to retrace steps
dusk falling	into night
night sounds	stars emerging
owls calling	rodent rustle
bittern booming	dark shape
not finding	turning back

Now Considering y^t it was my dismal fate
for to repent I Thought it now to late

In
a forest
of similarities
we find our path by slight distinctions
the aberrant, the taller tree
lush moonferns beside a spring
a slight displacement
a witch's broom
a tree's growth slowed by fire scorch
a line of fire
a paler green in slightly younger spruce
except

when strangers are
in strange uncertainty,
dark forests' certain strangeness,

nothing is knowable

the echoes taunt
seem to "Holloa!" assuredly
in willows, cinquefoils, Labrador tea
cougar, wolverine, or bear
or some unknown worse thing rustles:
I must be still:
friends'll shout:
I must shout

And once y^t in my travels I was left behind
Which struck fear & terror into me

Being lost	knowing
where you seem	to be
ignorant	where the others
wandering	ahead
plunging on	think you ahead
dissembling	laughing at fear
grievance, grief, gratitude	assume an attitude
no longer figure	in sullen valour

Because I was alone & no friend could find

alone	remembering
the lost	aimlessly
in circles	stumbling
come upon their own fear	snaring themselves
fatally	in a question

But still I was resolved this same Country for to see

Fixed, still	waiting
quarry	seeks you
as you	seek it

For many times I have often been oppresst
With fears & Cares y^t I could not take my rest

lank after long walking the tendons chafe,
in the cold the rib cage caves,
in snow stumbling,
partaking in ritual and blaspheming,
belly weak after long hunger,
eating the dogs,
gluttony in the after-kill excess,
belly's sore swelling
heaving in sickness,
damp powder, wet moccasins,
feet blue cold beside the ashen embers,
blindness in the light after the storm,
an all-white vacancy
in whiteness lost
lost
in the wrong language speaking
                          knives flash

reverting to English,
ground blizzards,
the stench of the middens by noon thaw,
maggots crawling from the roasting meat,
bears devour carrion,
silence overwhelming
and at my side
                              her
                    the long night
              lengthening nights and
        always in strength and in warmth

Impossible, impassible winter walls us,
return to the fort now a failure
kindling their laughter

Soft bog sucks moccasins by the beaked sedge,
ducks through the pondweed emerge,
mudroots in their bills,
wind sways the long-stalked cattails drying,
the bright eyes of muskrats gleam at the water's edge.

Woods thin,
temper thins,
                    untempered muscles
                    twitch under skin

The women gather the last berries for pemmican:
autumn rots, decays.

The ground begins for to be dry with wood
Poplo & birch with ash thats very good
For the Natives of that place wch knows
No use of Better than their wooden Bows
According to ye use & custom of this place

A weapon of dexterity and grace,
supple from summers' faster growth and hard
and tight from winters'; by bole of branch unmarred;
in fall selected for the straightest bough,
shaped to a thumb's thickness where a left hand now
holds it erect, but narrowing to its ends
where harp-strung sinew tightens, bends
its flexing, tautens it to muscles' tension
against their own, as if their own intention
hewed their weapon from their thews; its swift
and pointed sapling arrow the bow can lift
a tree's height in arc and plummet from that height
into a moose's heart, darkening its flight;
sustains their enmity they will not cease.

In September I brought these Natives to a peace

no willows wail
nor night wind rises

But I had no sooner from those Natives turnd my back
Some of the home Indians came upon their track

moccasin silent
the blade silent

69

And for old grudges & their minds to fill
Came up with them Six tents of w^(ch) they kill'd

knife-slit throats
the warm blood flows
men's and women's

This ill news kept secrett was from me

their gore is the same

Nor none of those home Indians did I see

whispering in the reeds

Untill that they their murder all had done
And the Chief acter was he y^(ts) call ye Sun

It better were   he ran away
as history held   for centuries

Thus it continues till you leave ye woods behind
And then you have beast of severall kind
The one is a black a Buffillo great
whose size would call forth titan's tumult
summoning trumpeted speeches from dumb mouths
and in his majesty the thunderheads
roil in his cumulus hulking shoulders' mass
of curls that become the robe in winter will
sustain us in the sharp winds' blast;
his great horned head is higher than mine own
and bears his pride, even when lazily he grazes
the eared grass, champing delicately;

then when he rolls the dust he raises
darkens the sky; he snorts like bellows in a forge;
he drums in running like the sound of deep waves
pounding on the shores of this inland sea of grass;
in spring their bodies filled the rivers
and on the banks their bodies piled up
and ravens sat and ate their eyes and brains.

At the last of summer's false return the bison
clouded the plain turned sky unto horizon
and at their burrows' entrances the squirrels
awaited licks of wind, dustdevil whirls,
to sully the yellow, golden, pale blue flowers
of asters, ragweed, bergamot in hours
drying, reseeding this land "of good report,"
so pale, once bountiful, unlike the fort
I left in spring's onset to undertake
this inland journey for my masters' sake.

Trusting still unto my masters Consideration
Hoping they will Except of this my small Relation
Which here I have pend & still will Justifie
Concerning of those Indians & their Country

Rarely is it given to a man to find
a continent to which his homeland's blind,
and wander in it freely two swift years
of joy and awe and wonder, yet in fears
he'll not return; and carefree yet, unheeding
terror, disentangle what is needing:
commerce, comfort, shelter, peace in the land,
all of which the Indians little understand.

But still I was resolved this same Country for to see

Although through many dangers I did pass
Hoped still to undergo y^m at the Last

Mind is	prairie
wide and trackless	earth and air
overwhelms	inculcate
us	a calculus of
despairing	moving
as	homunculi
under	accumulate
clouds	the unanswerable
uncontained metaphor	mind
prairie is	doubt
coursed	by rivers
shaped	by glaciers
asundered	by wind
till what is left	diminishes
is primacy	and rebegins
atoms of	thought
irreducibility	conjoins
in	concept
plain	speech
force	utterance
what he feels	must express itself
prosaically	in poetry
as later	secrets
he wrote	in Indian tongue

they have but two or three Words in a song
& they observe to keep time along with him
y^t is ye leader of ye song
for Every man maketh his own songs
by vertue of w^t he dreams of

systole

golden autumn
shrinks seed

diastole

rose hips wrinkle
leaf mulch

systole

burnt red
willow tips

diastole

cold clarity
in the stream

systole

aspen ignite
yellow, birch yellow

diastole

grassyellow, passing yellow
burnished willow

systole

pigeons shot
wood sounds dying

diastole

mourning, soughing
lowing, moaning

systole

crowd crows
raucous, murderous

diastole

eve of migration
owls' ululation

systole

piebald ermine
weasels vary

diastole

```
                    geese vee
                    hare vary

systole
                    hawks depart
                    bears den
                                                        diastole

                    quietus
                    silence
systole
                    distance
                    water
                                                        diastole
```

The tracing wavering of a skipping pen
on frail and fraying, ancient, greying paper—
a splotched gooseberry on snow

    Distance from hence by Judgement at ye lest
    From ye house six hundred miles southwest

Nothing is knowable   except uncertainty

His direction known   whence did he come

Place unknown   when he was there

& at ye Conclusion of every song
they give thanks all in general to him
y^t ye song belongs too
So likewise if any one hath crost or vext them
y^t they owe him any grudge
they will pretend to set w^t they dream of to work
& it shall kill the offender at his pleasure

Trace
place of beginning   place of end
and
the one who returns   is not who went out
                    circuit incomplete
He disappears   gains momentum, escapes
vanishes   in the ways of likeness
                              is lost

                    Define thyself
              consider thy autumns
                    keep silence

The muskrat inhale the bubbles, faces beneath the ice,
then back down into the black water vanish;
loon swimming in a shrinking circle of closing ice
bargain till the room for taking flight is gone;
a cacophony of scavengers—jays, ravens, coyotes, carcajous—
argue over the scraps of the wolves' kill.

                    (Listen:)
              the air is quiet
                    (Listen:)
              the melody attenuates
              largo notes fragmenting
              drone   dirge
              concealing lethargy

life's almost silent   music's yet in silence
shapes silence   in which it is at rest
sweet

                                             spontaneous
                    silence

                              75

Insurgent wave, ocean journey, the hyperboreal strait

lost in time   in wilderness unending
lost in world   in time expanding
lost   becoming
                    something other
                forgotten and reclaimed

Etomomi, its two ways clear
South to Assiniboine, north to Red Deer

            The river flows both ways

where it reverses   unexplorably shifts

great eddies wheeling
capture flotsam
suspend it at the torrents' edges
an unstill point that stays
borne in current by the current
stilling time in motions' space
against the frisson of the flowing
while whirling
smaller eddies whirl around
and at their edges
still smaller
until still points of spinning
nothing
nothing turn and wheel away

Time vanishes   in the flow of metaphor

Tone slows   lean in richness

margin   zone of grey   disappearance   horizon   fade

simultaneity   similarity

plucked into present
from behind grey castle walls
bleak backdrop to Irish fields
where cattle champ
a castle kept
secrets
and profits from the furs

synchronicity   spontaneity

systole
                    the bright secret
                                            diastole

plangent in bushes   cabinet or closet
the dry leaves   paper rustlings
crabbed letters in an old hand   the writing decipherable
two centuries   the suppression
memory of Dobbs   willing to conceal but
not smashing the link   that would reveal
the lad, nineteen   difficult to remember
                                                in the stature

accomplishing   just
coming back alive   not failing in commerce

Red blood the red water
flowing in the runnelled surface
ripples, swells
in standing waves and ice
coats the boulders

changing the shapeless torrent of life into a discrete quantity

language is a vehicle   the universe decrees
for its description   creating spaces
for another space   to exist
silence between utterances   in space
in which are acts   acts begetting facts
in which words form   totem, factotum
fact, act, fiction   the thing made
in space   a journey made
made   journeyman's creation
time   isolating
into Autumn   the declining   sun
narrows   river   day by day
before   after
here and   there
are   abstracts
without   meaning
there is a point   at which
something is   nothing
and nothing   is   something
clear water   at sunset   encased
silver ice   sluggish   .beneath mica
stored willows   wavering   the current
wind wane   leaf gold   near stillness

black blossoms   rose hips   the flatness

ground mist   glisten   deer listen

berry-eating bear   in the cool   aspen

in the dark   spruce   forest

primeval   mind   until

one by one   the stars   appear

eldritch spruce   silhouette   fantasies

magnify   the slipping   sky

owl calling   season   eyes

in the darkness   staring

query   quarry   keenly

qwho   quiver

shivering   taut

drum   snare   canopy

singing   chant

beyond   meaning

Part y^e Third
Nivation

History begins in Novel and ends in Essay . . .
—MACAULAY, "HISTORY AND LITERATURE"

Winter is wolf waiting for man to falter;
lowing wind, flowing moon, blowing snow;
o stray and wandering words, stay
        with me a while

O strange, bewildering thoughts
bred of the tempest, borne by the storm
born of winter

      The blue wolf howls

The savage faces of the land,
masks of fir, eyes of ice and mystery
salvage my spars

      The spruce tree cracks

Yet above me, over reader as over writer,
wheel the sustaining stars

      O God, be merciful

Sparks rise in the fire's night flare;
warmth and memory cling to the embers.

The wind is singing in a woman's voice,
dark and mysterious is the wind;
the land lies fertile yielding to me,
the sun is silver and the sky is bright,
and I am called by the wind to the land,
the wind which is singing in a woman's voice
and the land that lies like a woman lying
beneath the sun which burns in the air
bared to the warmth of the hovering sun
which clings like a burr in the sky,
and the wind is singing, soft as moaning—
"There is a meaning, meaning meaning"
soft in the hush of summer wind
soft as the sweetgrass flows like hair
in the wind that hesitates in its harmony
ever returning as a memory,
waving and washing the clouds and sky,
brushing the cottonwoods under the sun;
wishing wind will come as a woman,
soft as fair as sun of summer and brushing
as the wind is hushing a soft and summer day.

Summer and winter, river and wind:
I am adrift on smoke;
wind that between the nunatuks blew
blows where the ice is gone.

Here Oomingmuk persists the pale red dawn,
raises the bearded one his hornwall head,
blue eyes searching through the arctic smoke,
for over the long night's gulf
he hears the rising howl of a wolf.

Time is rising on the fire
into the winter night;
summer and winter, fire and smoke,
my eyes discern no light.

The ice plate wanes
and the mammoths and mastodons, tapirs and mylodons,
tigers and horses fall on the bier of time;
and only the muskox lives on the arctic edge
where to the howl of the wolf and the wind
he raises his ancient head.
Fluid in summer with the grass he flows with,
in lichen patina on ancient rock;
in winter bull and herd are one.

June 25th	*forc'd ashore by ye Ice*
1689	*now we Judged our selves to be about 20 Leagues*
	from Churchill River
ye 29th	*This days Journey most part ponds & hills . . .*
Thursday	*found an old Cannoe of those northern Indians*
	abundance of Musketers
ye 30th	*travelled all within Land it being all hills*
friday	*& more barren then before*
	ye hills being all stones wth a coat of moss over y^m
July	*it Raind hard*
ye 2^d	*having no shelter but ye heavens for a Cannope*
Sunday	*nor no wood to make a fire*

Bending north to summer's sill, winter's threshold
                    face to face

ye 9th	*Setting forward good weather*
sunday	*& going as it were on a Bowling green*
	in ye Evening spyded Two Buffillo
	left our things & pursued y^m
	we Kill'd one
	they are ill shapen beast
	their Body being bigger than an ox
	leg & foot like ye same
	but not half so long a long neck & head a hog
	their Horns not growing like other Beast
	but Joyn together upon their forehead
	& so come down ye side of their head & turn up
	till ye tips be Even wth ye Buts
	their Hair is near a foot long

On the wind the howl of the wolves,
their circle pack and the snow hard, crusted, and the wind:
       always the wail on the wind.

Borne to the bearded ones, wail within wail,
is the mingled odour of fear and hunger,
and the herd of muskoxen, heads in the lee of the storm,
snow coning about the hollows of their bulk, wait,
hearing the keening, turn toward struggle in shadow.

      The form of the enemy is memory,
      recollection, not form,
      forced into shape by instinct's code,
      the old intrinsic coping within drama.

Round and insistent is the dream and the ring
of the herd and the pack and the rising wind;
the barrier of buttress behind which instinct dwells,
guard ring of bulls about cows and calves.

The tyranny of instinct fails.
Bulls, calves, cows, all fall

What wolves are these,
striking and biting from unseen hills?

Phalanx of instinct fails.

Smoke traces smoke;
seek smoke and find flare.

It had been undertaken to send *the boy Henry Kelsey*
to Churchill River with Thomas Savage because . . .
he is a very active Lad delighting much in Indians Company
being never better pleased than when
he is Travelling amongst them

Who recognized the   stranger   returned?

Kelsey *was not sensable of ye dangers.*
Those to whom he reported now were strangers.

Two summers since,
a winter in the fort between,
now wintering darkness.
Who could be aught except insensible?
Look back to the boyhood now you are beyond:
you discerned it, enriched it, lived it
when your beard was no darker than
the land of little sticks in sifting snow.

    In 83 I went out in ye ship Lucy Jno outlaw command^r
    an ocean's breadth between your home and land

in 88 after 3 indians being employ'd for great rewards
to carry letters from hays river to new severn   they return'd
wthout performing ye business altho paid
then was I sent wth an indian boy
& in a month return'd wth answers

Memory surges as the water in the wake of the canoe,
veering scintillas away from the prow;
the darkness opens now:

                   In 89 Capt James young
put me & ye same Indian boy ashore
to ye N^o ward of Churchill river
in order to bring to a commerce ye N^othern indians
but we saw none altho we travell'd above 200 miles
in search of y^m : finding darkness in the summer

Perhaps it should stand: "I ran away."
It might as well have been.
Ran to the mystery the shore concealed,
ran to the forest darkness, or from Geyer and his punishment,
as some would say, upon some *Boyish misbehaviour* chastised, I fled
and Geyer made *a Merit* of my *going up*
which Geyer undertook it was his own idea.

To him to whom the wind has sung orders mean little.
Honour I accorded his lord shagginess,
peering from beneath his hornbrow eminence,
serene in the loneliness of the unpeopled barren,
awe and respect as for no man.

Oomingmuk
bearded, sage, wise, and woeborn
wears the cloak of winter's hovering
waiting wolves
the forming of the ring
the closing of the ring
about the ring
Oomingmuk
bearded one
with the others
his head raises
into the wind whine
hearkens the tightening of
one of many circles

As rivers
etch patterns
time etched response in
Oomingmuk
obdurate, obstinate

and England
Kelsey, died
in you when you
beheld him
and you *kill'd one*

Oomingmuk lies
unmoving in a puddle of blood
oozing into tundra
redder than lichen
the lichens soaking
a precious wetness

Above the land always death hovers;
death and the barrens lie like lovers
intertwined, spent of their desire;
but the barrens knew not death as fire.

Time, depth, and distance fall away;
a cozened reader in a future age
will find a calmness in a rage
of rivers flouting time and space,
in meeting wildness face to face.

I stand in the haggard wind of winter,
turbulent air and colder times,
considering the depths of nights,
the distance travelled, the stars' cold light,
the muteness of my mouth where language fell away from me
until my silence forced me to reach
for any utterance, any speech
my chafed hand might render :
>   *Now Reader Read for I am well assur'd*
>   Winter has forted us, and us immur'd
>   *Thou dost not know the hardships I endur'd*

It is a beginning;
the wind is singing,
fire is dying:
the voice of the land is the wind,
the wind is the voice of the land, and

when you have heard the wind and its singing,
you shall have begun to understand.

Interlude
Dreambearer

In more than arctic darkness
no day begins as the long day begins

no music moves
where no thing moves
where nothing is
but the dream of the bear is dreamt

no word moves
as the great bear's mind forms in night
in cold beyond cold
the absolute
stillness
the world's long climb to daylight and delight
begins

form   mind   bear   idea   dream
breaking while a thought breaks
the word moves within the dark
the bear's form is borne in the great bear's mind

the void
begins to heave
weight and mass
slowly and critically
coalesce

form and idea
collide and collapse

thc first trickling warmth

a word, a wind
breath, motion, swift light
hurled in a widening arc
thrusts through the dark
in the slow coition of universe
and the world's conception
in the wind behind the word
in an archaic dream

The sun is a fiction
under the rim of white light in indigo
the pale pink hope of warmth
spirit of rock
storms of creation
cloud   chaos   music   words   dreams
in white fragmenting light

beneath the stars
that one by one
form while the word is light and
move through mind to light and shape

out of the sleeping dreambearing night

Part ye Fourth
Flensing

. . . one might almost say that metonomy corresponds to
the order of events, metaphor to the order of structure.
—LÉVI-STRAUSS, *Totemism*

Sweat flecks the tawny hide, urging
the ecstasy the buck dies in, surging
ecstasy, crumbling on its legs splaying,
slaughter's dreary darkness replacing
    the surgent rapture.

    The larynx tightens; the word is drawn back;
    before the utterance is thrown, the breath is drawn;
    the heart's cords and the hand's tendons tighten;
    song brims in the tension of silence.

    Let my song fly; the arrow is true.

If at any time they are in want of victuals
they will fit a young man out wth something of their own making
    as it may be half a dozen peruant stones
    wch they have gott from ye factory
    or Else a pipe steam
now these pruant stones they scrape smooth & burn spots,
    or ye shape of any thing as their fancy leads y^m
now if happens y^t this young man wch is fitted out
should kill a Beast y^t day
then they will impute it to ye things he carried about him
    & so it passes for a God Ever afterwards

The blade scores the soft belly flesh
and the guts of the buck spill out;
the knife flickers by the legs' tendons
revealing the pale yellow wax of fat.

After winter's hunger slaked by small birds only,
after the trials of hunting on spring's collapsing snow,
after the ribs of spring poking lankly,
                    summer seems good

Midsummer, sixteen hundred ninety one
ye floods past ye Snow eat by ye Sun
Near to Starvation obtaining from ye Govr
ye powder shott Tobacco for our Endeavour
wch items for all of which I asked
As necessary for my inland task
We sett out again seeking for to find
ye Stone Indians being ten days travell behind
at Deerings point and by cannoes we past
By creeks and brooks, ponds deepe in grass
wch like our English oats is ear'd
Leaving our cannoes Inland we veer'd
& made an hole as storehouse in ye Ground
wch when we pass hence next Spring will be found
A Bagg of Powder Tobacco & ye nettline
One tin show a hatchet & 2 skains of twine
In a rundlett wch in ye Ground we placed
& abandonned in our Hunger & our Hast
For to journey further & to track ye Stones
Who by Evidence of ye scraps & Bones
Were 4 days only farr in front of us
& better victualled so catch up we must
In 9 days trek we came up with y^m at last

After heavy mossy going we had past
& they had kill'd both swans & muse
ye Chief gave me ye Gut he had cut loose

But now no Beast they kill
but some part or other is allotted for mans meat
wch ye women are not to tast of upon no acco^t. . .
by reason they think it will be a hindrance
to their Killing any more Beast
*   nay if a woman should eat any of this mans meat*
wch is called in their language Cuttawatchetaugan
& fall sick in a year or 2 afterwards & dye
they will not stick to say it y^t kill'd her
for all it was so long ago she eat it

Now if they have a mind for to make a feast
they will pitch a tent on purpose
& after y^t ye tent is made & fixt
then no woman Kind y^t hath a husband
*   or is known to have been concern'd wth a man*
must not come within the door of ye tent afore^{sd}

The gore warms stiff fingers,
palpable intestines fall in black heaps
on the crimsonned snow;
a foreleg jerks a last twitch.
The knife dances in glints
severing integuments and the hide's off-gloving
reveals a more naked, strangely dry and gangling body;
the blood deserting the fallen body
drips into baskets placed there as catchbasins
and frost invades the moments before warm tissue.

A word spumes on the baby's lips; the child does not cry;
words bubble on the rocks of rapids; incoherent murmuring;
words echo in the waking dream.
Drum tight tension: the forming words.

concerning their singing of their songs
& from whence they think they have y^m
    those that they reckon Chiefly for gods
    are Beast and fowl
    But of all Beast ye Buffillo
    & of all fowls ye voulter & ye Eagle
    wch they say they dream of in their sleep
    & it relates to y^m w^t they shall say when they sing
    & by y^t means whatsoever they ask or require
    will be granted or given y^m
    wch by often making use of it
    sometimes happens to fall out Right as they say
    & for y^t one time
    it will pass for a truth y^t he hath a familiar
    although he hath told never so many lies before

The drying bubbles blacken the snow;
the frame-stretched hide tautens;
the strands of tendon dry;
the spitted legs roast.

Our hungry bellyes were fill'd at great Feast
For now there was no want of fowl or Beast
Very glad were they y^t I had return'd
And by my promise else were it learn'd
I was dead the Nayhathaways w^d murder y^m
& Master of ye Feast I was for I had come

then ye master of ye tent & one or two more
goeth in & Cutteth out a place for ye fire
about three foot square in ye middle of ye tent
& then ye fire being made they take a little sweet grass
& lay at every corner of ye said square
& then putting fire to it they perfume the tent so
Making a long speech wish all health & happiness
   both to founders & confounders

One year's cycle spent;
dawn startled our onset
renewing us

Rested & wth pigeons & muse well fed
Proceeded we to ye river y^t is Blood read
Where I should talk with ye Naywatame
y^t had strong fear of harm in meeting me
For they 3 Nayhathaway women kill'd
A spring before and fear of revenge y^m fill'd

So far I have spoken concerning of the spoil
And now will give acco^t of that same Country soile
Which hither part is very thick of wood
Affords small nutts wth little cherryes very good
Through heathy barren land in fields we pitch
y^t hath no fir but by fine groves of Poplo is enricht

The sun glimmers on the shores of that broad plain

One Indian lay adying and withall
A murmuring for warrs among y^m was ye call
In counsel said I to ye elder Dons
Y^t was not ye way to use ye English guns

   a smile radiates a face
   brightening eyes' bleak hollows

& so by their singing
will pretend to know w^t ye firmament of heaven is made of
nay some Indians wch I have discoursed with
has told me they have been there & seen it
so likewise another has told me
y^t he had been so near to ye sun at ye going down
y^t he could take hold of it when it Cut ye Horrizon

Not knowing wch could Conquer Life or Death
Lay still and waited with held breath
Till y^t he died and then his body burn'd
& buried we made new camp and turn'd
They holding y^t it was not good to stay
Where y^t one died according to their way

Every man maketh his own songs by vertue of w^t he dreams of
as I have said before

And the dream of the bear is dreamt:

Spirit
solitary
bearer of darkness
in man's sleep his grunting
his silver-dark pelt at the edges
melts
at the edge of sleep out of the darkness
robing him in thick-rilled silver
surmounting
the hump of his shoulders
down to the talons of his claws

Ride on the back of the great humped bear
to the stars in the night of the vast dark's sphere

Out of dream darkness and running
the bear pursuing the dreamer running
through silver-slipping birches waits
till the dreamer slipping falls

and in the eyes of the bear's great head
is reflected the diminishing realm he withdraws from,
driven back and retreating until

> a high chill wind
> on small willows
> blows cloud wisps
> the high silver clouds
> and the rider
> upon and within the
> bear
> sees
> the world smaller

Bear, having borne him in his becoming the bear's eyes,
stands and surveys the sources of fear's pungence and terror.

Out of the heap of sleep
the breath of death bloody and bubbling
in the half-light of memory
the great bear strides across the sky.

> The hills, the clouds, the poplar bluffs
> he cannot reduce to parables of death
> from the edge where he now sees
> a bold simplicity where he finds himself standing

> alone

Pitcht to ye outtermost Edge of ye woods
Where y^t ye silver haired Great Bear broods
His skin to gett I have used all ye ways I can
He is mans food & he makes food of man
His hide they would not me it preserve
But said it was a god & they should Starve
Neither white nor black like ye common Bear
But more like unto y^t our English Hare
Also Buffillo like the English ox their horns
Unlike those y^t to N^otharward are born
We were in all now eighty tents
Together now on y^t our going hence
& full 200 of us proceeding at the least
To the woods y^t lyeth along West and East
Which at last we reached & there perforce
Y^e men requested y^t I let them to the warrs
W^ch I forbade the Govern^r would not it allow
But I y^m would reward should they seek now
Y^e Naywatane poets & if y^t they be found
Here where y^t ye Beavour do abound
September ye 1st their Enemies land we near'd
With 8 Indians who y^m greatly fear'd
& fill'd me with dread Anticipation
Of speaking with y^m and Interpretation
At morn & crying out just like the Crane
Young scouts arrived the Enemy they'd seen
& as if forJoy they had been stobb'd
Y^e old men Served ye steam and sobb'd
While y^t ye young men sat without a sound
Showing y^m ye old Arrows they had found
Counselled I again they should not to ye wars
Y^e Comp^y preferring Peace to use of Force
But all my arguements little prevailed
For they believed the rout they sought availed

Four Strangers of the Naywatame poets
Came wch received kindly gave us notice
Of where their Capt was and so I went
To him and parleyed with him in his tent
& all ye Arguements then with him made
Concerning all ye Advantages of ye Trade
Saying he should forget his men were kill'd
Y^t were his Trade with us fulfill'd
We English should prevent it going further
& presented him with Gifts moreover
A coat & sash beads awls and whatnot
Tobacco & a gun wth Powder and some shot
Y^t pleased him well indeed & thus he said
My amends were enough for y^m his dead

                  In the heat haze
                    the sun rises
                 and the sun sets
                   streams gather
                and flow to the sea

                  In the heat haze
              mirage magnifies space
             it is time to turn back now
          beyond the bright flare of the day
                to the foil of darkness

            It is time to make the signs

The long swept grass gathered and dried; the sweet grass sustaining;
The long sweet grass burning sweetens the air with its smoke:
The pipe brims with the dried leaves of bearberry; seeds and sweet
    herbs in a mound on a flat, scorched rock:
Coarse fingers bear coals from the fire, small coals igniting the leaves
    grasses, seeds:
He calls through the haze of the tent: they enter and sit on a hide:
His fingers lift an ember which he places in the bowl of the pipe,
    and the lit pipe he passes to the first of them who
    turns its stem in his fingers; the bowl toward him, he turns the
    stem to the northeast, the fort, where the old man has directed it:
Where the old man directs, he points the stem to the point of the
    rising sun:
Where the old man directs, he turns it south to where the sun rises
    highest:
Then to the sun's setting point, where the sun rests:
Tendrils of smoke cling in closedness as the old one another ember
    places in the bowl:
The second who takes it repeats the points of the compass, pausing
    and passing it:
Pausing and passing; taking and turning:
Sweet is the smoke, silent the ceremony till all have taken the pipe.

Sweet are the berries: we sing and rejoice in our singing.

I stand
in the middle
of the long grass
I turn
to the north and east
where the river flows
I turn
beneath the sun at noon
turn
to the ground
to the sky
draw
the sweet breath of the air
into my chest
and
like a giant heart ebb and flow with wind
and with seasons

It is time to turn back; time to turn from the mysteries; the hunt
    is over.
At the sun's rising my shadow yearned itself into the tall grass:
At noon my shadow was short; I was unaware of my shadow:
Now in the dusk my shadow stretches and points toward home:
We will rise and walk early into the sun with the sun behind us
    when day is done.
About the lone bear at the edge of the woods who nudged a stump
    over to eat its grubs a noose of the sun tightens.

This plain affords nothing but Beast & grass
And over it in three days time we past
Getting into y^e woods on the other side
It being about forty six miles wide
This wood is poplo ridges with small ponds of water
There is beavour in abundance but no Otter
With plains & ridges in the Country throughout
Their Enemies many whom they cannot rout
But now of late they hunt their Enemies
And with our English guns do make y^m flie

(I saw her with another woman;
like beaver kittens they were playing
beside the bank of the pond's still water,
splashing and raising a flight of ducklings,
then clambering up the slick grass and resting,
reclining and lying in the late summer warmth;
my heart was wandering with my mind.)

At deerings point after the frost
I set up their a Certain Cross
In token of my being there
Cut out on it ye date of year
And Likewise for to veryfie the same
Added to it my master sir Edward deerings name

Goldenrod, silverwood, water calla, dragonhead,
bunchberry, ragwort, paintbrush, and sedge,
Indian pipe, meadow rue, bur-reed, silverthread,
hornwort: growing at the water's edge.

Bog myrtle, sun dew, bracken and pincherries,
pitcher plants, touch-me-not, milfoil and brome,
twinflowers, bishop's cap, running pine, cloudberries:
garland the one who returns slowly home.

Frost fins the bog;
squirrels chatter noisomely;
And so another autumn, winter, long winter.

At Deerings point ye following spring
Y^e Naywatame chief having promised to bring
Down in aboundance ye Beavour pelts
For Trading gunns, powder and all else
All of wch y^t ye Captn & I did Agree
Eager our Endeavours fruit to see
At ye place of ye Resortance
Upon wch I had place a great Importance
But in ye Spring failed they to arrive
W^{ch} means our Goal we did not achieve
Y^e reason for ye failure being so
Y^t wch we hoped they would forego
After we had parted from ye Naywatame

An event I anticipated did dismay me
W^{ch} was y^t secretly ye Nayhathaway
Came up and two of y^m did slay
W^{ch} a new terror struck into y^m
Y^t they would not be let back again
If y^t they should leave to Deerings Point
All of my labours then was quite disjoint
Y^e Chief sent to me a pipe & steam
Of his own making wch I accepted y^m
& in return I sent him then a Piece
Of Tobacco from ye House with Pleas
He w^d come down ye following Year
Overcoming in desire for Trade his Fear

Having no more to trouble you wth all I am
Sir your most obedient & faithfull Servt at Command
Henry Kelsey

Two Notes

In the autumn of 1967, free from a master's thesis, I started a poem about muskoxen. I maundered through that winter while I was a student at Stanford, provoked at whiles by Linda who believed no such animal could exist nor that it could fascinate anyone. In 1968's autumn, home in Banff, I took up the notes for the poem, and read some more, finding that Henry Kelsey had been the first to describe the pleistocene relic. Even more interesting, he had been the first English poet of the Canadian prairies, an ancestral voice. "Poet?" I liked him, thought his poetry doggerel. I thought to do a send-up of him. But, as I reread him, I kept hearing in his poem the genuine. He took over the poem about the muskox. The poem began to shape itself into epic. My academic work on the medieval poem *Pearl* started to inform what I was doing: I would, like the jeweller of that poem, put his poem into a new setting. Hence "homage."

Kelsey in 1690 took his journey to the plains and wrote his couplets about that trip upstream. The rest of his journal consists of brief notes. In finishing my poem I took his notes and finished for him his journey in poetry in my part IV, "Flensing." The reader of *Homage, Henry Kelsey* may distinguish his text from mine, for his is in italics throughout. His text is taken from *The Kelsey Papers,* edited by Arthur G. Doughty and Chester Martin.

In 1971, John Orrell presented the first two parts of *Homage, Henry Kelsey* in *White Pelican* and Andy Suknaski reprinted one of those in his *Elfinplot.* In 1973 what eventually became "Interlude: Dreambearer" appeared in *Three* (Noble, Thompson, Whyte; Banff: Summerthought). In 1976, while I was writing a poem about Leslie Reid, a technical innovation occured in one of my poems that led to the *technopaegnia* of *Open Spaces,* an exhibition and book of poems shaped about a "hole," (Peter Whyte Foundation, Banff: 1977). The space, and a reading of Octavio Paz' "Sun Stone" provided the technical means to shape the rest of the poem, and in the autumn of '76 I drafted it out.

In April, 1978 I passed the manuscript on to David Arnason of Turnstone, and later heard from Robert Enright that the poem was going to be published. In the meanwhile in Regina in November, 1978, Kristjana Gunnars heard me read from *Kelsey* and requested a portion of it for *Freelance,* the magazine of the Saskatchewan Writers' Guild she was then editing. I rewrote for her what had by then become Part II, and it appeared in February, 1979.

The day before Christmas, 1980, I received the text back, heavily and excellently noted and tightened by Wayne Tefs, my Turnstone editor. In early 1981 I reread, for the first time in five years, the entire text, taking a lot of Wayne's advice, but gripping some portions he suggested removing. Kelsey and I got lost again, more than once, but I think Kelsey has taken me through his ultimate, for me, transformations.

Finally it remains to be noted that about the time I was setting out on the Kelsey Trail, Dennis Burton, in my opinion one of Canada's most important artists, was also on the trail, undertaking a commission from the Post Office to design the commemorative stamp which appeared in 1970, the three hundredth anniversary of Kelsey's birth (and the Hudson's Bay Company). In 1976 I met Dennis, and then, it seems so long ago, he promised to provide drawings for the text if the poem ever found a publisher. Dennis has had a free hand in his renderings, for he understands Henry Kelsey better than any artist in Canada.

—*Jon Whyte*

THE FELLS *of* BRIGHTNESS: SOME FITTES *and* STARTS
Preface

The Fells of Brightness, which is to say "Assine Watche," directly translated from Cree, "brilliant mountains," the Rockies; volume 1, *Some Fittes and Starts,* which is to say "several cantos and beginnings or surprises." But "fell" is also a folded edge of cloth or textile (which word we derive from the Latin for "text") and "fitte," we find, is a thread weavers used to mark a day's text-making, hence a "hem mark"; and thus "fell" and "fitte" both connote a raised ridge of text, the mountains ranged or arranged.

These notes to get you over the foothills and into the text. I am not purposefully obscure; it would just seem that way. *"The Fells of Brightness"* was a title for an essay on the pioneer Banff photographer Byron Harmon; Oxford found it too rich and called the essay "An Appreciation," freeing it for another use.

The poem's genesis is in my being born and raised in Banff, and in a first leap at a long poem about the Rockies in 1957 when I cast about for a subject big enough for a long poem. I had that year read *Towards the Last Spike* and, if E.J. Pratt could write a poem as long as the CPR, I would write a poem big as a mountain. The Frank Slide was my theme. I knew nothing about it. I've lost or, more likely, thrown away any fragments of that first attempt at epic, but I recall I imitated stout Anglo-Saxon tetrameter. The only line I remember is a description of the mountain about to fall, "like a puma perched upon a pine." Chaucer's parody of alliterative verse in Sir Thopas' Tale trounced such heavy-handed four-point consonance.

I learned English fairly well and crafted poetry variously but, upon returning to Banff in 1968, I began for the first time in a decade to write again about this place. *Homage, Henry Kelsey* [1] intervened, yet one might read it as prologue to *The Fells,* for it incorporates history, myth, landscape, a literary past, and is a foray into "anatomical epic," lying like the prairies before the mountains. Shorter poems—600 to 800 lines; these

---

1   *Homage, Henry Kelsey.* Turnstone Press, Winnipeg, 1981.

things are relative—on narratives in Rockies settings[2] were warming-up exercises. In 1977 I began *The Fells* with the assistance of a Canada Council grant. In 1979 I became fully employed and publishers, ever watchful of such goings on, began to request manuscripts. Shirley Neuman, editor of this and my prior book with Longspoon Press, *Gallimaufry*, selected a portion of *The Fells* for inclusion in that book. I have since rewritten that fragment, taking advantage of the typographic realizations I and David Carr had worked out for *Homage, Henry Kelsey* which developed the play of space I had first published in *Open Spaces*,[3] a collection of technopaegnia, concrete, and emblematic poems. That playfulness had since become a liberating breakthrough for me. When Shirley expressed interest in Longspoons's publishing *Some Fittes and Starts,* I noted joyously her having married a book designer in April, 1982, and undertook to rewrite the poem to fulfill a book designer's nightmares.[4] Jorge Frascara, Shirley's husband, became designer for the volume and met several days ago a manuscript meant to invoke the full range of his talents. The results are in your hands. Frequently engaged in book design myself, I tend now to think of "the book," rather than of "the text." To Shirley and Jorge must go a large share of the credit for the realization of *Some Fittes and Starts.*

I forecast now five volumes of *The Fells,* each about the length of this volume, publication to follow leisurely and annually until 1987. *Some Fittes and Starts* is a genesis, establishing the cosmos, and autobiography, providing facts about the neighbourhood and bringing me into awareness; but it is the foundation of my poetics too, plumbing tropes and rhetoric and reestablishing the relevance of the great traditions of English poetry, allowing me the pleasure of bringing together all my love of *epos,* Hopkins, Marianne Moore, Byron, Al Purdy, Wordsworth and wordplay, play, history and old

---

2   "Paley" in *Three* (Charles Noble, J.O. Thompson, Jon Whyte), Summerthought, Banff, 1973; "The Agony of Mrs Stone" in *Matrix,* Vol 1, 1977, Lennoxville, P.Q., "WJP" in *Gallimaufry,* Longspoon Press, Edmonton, 1981.

3   *Open Spaces,* Peter Whyle Gallery, Whyte Foundation, Box 160, Banff, 1977.

4   I note with pleasure that Shirley was a student of mine at the University of Alberta when I taught Creative Writing there, 1966–67. Friends then, nothing has interrupted our affection for each other since. Who is mentor now? Mayhap Shirley.

gossip, and folklore and tale. Volume II, "Wenkchemna," will more fully develop themes only suggested here, a sort of "postlapsarian" trope of anisotropism in linguistic, geological and paleozoological terms, starting at the rock barrier which formed Moraine Lake, a result of the *lapsus* of quartzite from a mountain called the Tower of Babel, and then using the ten peaks of the Wenkchemna Range as indices to broadening experience. Volume III, not yet named, starts in Heraclitus and will be fluvial in form. Volume IV, also not yet named, will pick up autobiographical themes, and the ultimate volume, "Summits," will be a sort of *Paradiso,* hough I do not suggest life in Banff is *Purgatorio,* or that *Some Fittes and Starts* is *Inferno.*

The concerns of *The Fells* are numerous, but I can perhaps extract a few here to ease your way further into the matter. First is my interest in the form of the *anatomy,* which I prefer to define as "a panoptic treatment of a single subject, or a singular point of view brought to bear on a multiplicity of subjects." Second, and very obvious, is my joy in the richness of English. At one point in "Epeirogeny" I parody the old-fashioned post-modernists; post-modernism was nice while it lasted, I believe. Thank goodness it's over. The language was getting close to atrophying. Third is my dedication to culture and the idea of a cultured person who should, in the late days of the Twentieth Century, be cognizant of Wegener and what J. Tuzo Wilson has done for continental drift, but he should also be aware of Agassiz's contributions to glaciology, and Hutton's and Lyell's more classical geology; additionally he should be aware of the sorts of intelligent mysticism in Paz's *The Monkey Grammarian* (rather than, say, the slick marketing of Carlos Castaneda), the new cosmology of Stephen Hawking, (even if he cannot enunciate much of it), the rigourous imagination brought to bear upon the world by Carl Linnaeus, should have a bending awareness of structural anthropology, and he should be at least blithely aware of popular culture. Coming to the Rockies is not "The Way," but it is certainly among the ways, if only because the Rockies, like mountains everywhere, pose many of the problems of glaciology, geomorphology, ecology, and structuralism. (How did the mountains get carved? How did they get there in the first place? Why is it easier to survey transitions of life forms on a mountain side? Did Lyell and Hutton inform Claude Lévi-Strauss?) Additionally mountains invoke mythology (why did Jehovah talk to Moses on the mountain? Why did Zeus and the gang dwell on Olympus?) and obvious artistic problems (how do we perceive beauty in them in the onslaught of sentimentality?). My Rockies are, I hope, an archetype of anywhere, a complex of folk tale and anecdote, personal experience and Earth, a geography of climate, passion, and place. Should *The Fells* locate my *here,* then perhaps you'll find your *here* both here and everywhere, joyfully and delightfully.

Some illuminations of the book's dark areas I have endeavoured to provide in brief biographies of my kin and neighbours. Since a major segment of "Sources" concerns the Lake Louise region, the interested reader can pursue and peruse the book Carole Harmon and I assembled, *Lake Louise, A Diamond in the Wilderness.*[5] Some of the Whyte (White) family history is recapitulated in P*eter Whyte-Catharine Robb Whyte: A Commemorative Portfolio,*[6] available in some public libraries. *A Hunter of Peace*[7] includes the text of Mary T. S. Schäffer's *Old Indian Trails* and a biography of her by E. J. Hart which omits only one minor fact in her life: my mother visited Mary in 1931, met my father as a consequence of that visit, and ten years later I was a further consequence.

Jon Whyte
December 21, 1982

---

5   Altitude Publishing, Banff, 1982.

6   Whyte Foundation, Banff, 1980; edited by Jon Whyte.

7   *A Hunter of Peace,* The Whyte Foundation, Banff, 1981.

Sources

The fells:

        high meadows poigned on the spurs of massifs

        mountains   hills   the waste

        fell and dale   summing   summering

In April open

        lowland and fell   to broad and brightening
            the barrens   of snow

which   fellfield   brilliant   bears   above

        Sweep back your cape, o fell companion
        let moon light sky   and darken mystery

and   let the floods of spangling glory dapple
        fell, darkside traveller   time's cosener

        myth   history   family   the contumely

        flood   fell   stone shelves   and cobbles

Fell: all which I feel   find   form   fury
        fancy   fantasies   phantoms   phantasms

        all   upon   (which)   my eyes   fall

fell   darkness   fell

        and dreamborne   brilliance   bears

        some streamborne   secret   part
                                  art
                                  act
                                pact
                                past
                                fast
                                faster

                                          forward

Time's augmentation of the space distinguishes
defines
      :lines
      :particularities of aspect
                    :distinctions
                    :distinction
                                :an inside-
outedness
          making it as special
                           as what it limits
so by distinctions
          :mountains define
                :valleys define

        the Fells

      :high meadow margins   margins
      :hills hemming   hemming
      :mountains mooring   mooring
      :bens bordering   bordering
      :peaks patterning   patterning
      :summits summoning   summoning
      :Cairngorm loss   loss
           :loss of definition
           :selvage of self

unravelling   ragged   edges   fraying   tailors'   fells

"Take me to a mountain meadow," she dreamt
                      spoke
                      wrote
          (a clothed softness, like the pleached folds
          (concealing conception upsurgent mountains show;
          (the plaited stems of blossoms on her fingertips
                                  (entangled)
"and let us dawdle wandering beneath clouds' bellies,
"inspect the spiders' webbings strung from stem to stem;
"I'll ask the flowers' names, and know you know and hope
                                "you tell me them;"

(a naked brittleness: the sheer cliffs shorn,
(built to battlement and buttress as scraped
(by vale-deep ice that crept contained by cliff

(and carved them)

"our tongues inspect the honeyed secrets of the blossoms,
"nuzzle and tongue the styles' textures and their sweetness;
"lie, watch clouds play capers on the stony peaks and while

"the afternoon."

(A file of mountains, a rasp of dogteeth pikes
(seen from afar the Sawback seems, the torn horizon:
(will they wear us away? is that what draws us to them

(always?)

Fell:

the darkness

and in:

my dreams

summing up:

it adows me

brevity:

succinct summering

alpenglow:

and after

stillness

At its shadowed edge
the frayed shore of the dark forest
beside the lake shored
looking at the lake
its farside scene reflected
noting
in the darker parts in nearness
through the surface of the water
toward that which is thither
but the water nearer
the darker, clear bottom of the
lake
the branch-strewn bottom
of the lake
on which a scene is etched
a sketchy scene
and

for a shimmering moment   a thriceness   hold both
eyes   still

lake   reflection   lake bottom

lake   surface   shivers   shimmers

my eyes   fuzz   landscape   blurs

blurring   branches   lin surface   glacier

                                    reflections
                                        and
                                    perceptions

                    Memory skims the water, a water walker on its surface
                    walking on its reflection and on the tension brimming
                    molecule to molecule, force forming film and memory

                                **Four years old
                                ignorant of lakes
                            fascinated by the glassbrick
                            fracturing into repeating parts
                                the world that enters it
                                        reticulate
                            each repetition much the same
                        varying enough by each lens' parallax
                                        to pan
                                    by diffractions
                        a sort of Eadweard Muybridge vision
                                    of the world

                        the skeptic amateur of innocence
                                        admires
                        the rhythm repetition forms and forms

                        I sway my head with mazy motion
                                    side to side
                                to bend the world
                                panoramically around

                            the mayhem of the terrace
                                        shatters
                            impossibly into a sort of
                                        order

                                    learning

                        that which repeats satisfies:**

menorah of lodgepole pine; the set meringues of Rundle, Inglismaldie, Goat;
the sharksteeth peaks of Sawback; Ishbel's plates; the ripples on ponds;
the rhymes of Mother Goose, assonance, consonance; mares'-tails, mackerel-sky;
metronomes and pendulums; the pulse points on the carotids; Ravel's *Bolero;*
the wagging of a puppy's tail; dawns and daybreaks; days' similarities;
days' differences; the strata visible on Rundle and Cascade; the echoes;
echoes cusping phrases; phases of the moon; spaced boards of knotty pine;
and patterns of the knots themselves which bodied out the tree;
the lattice of linoleum irregular enough it needed hours and hours to figure out;
telephone pole symmetry, with forty poles marking miles; and railway ties,
the squares of concrete and the lines distinguishing sidewalks; plaids, setts,
and tartans; lines of fences; lengths of fences; the windows' arches
at the Cave and Basin; the cup hooks in the kitchen cupboard; second hands;
the cyclic path of hours, days, moons, months; and then, as years went by,
the winter-spring-summer-autumn repetition and the sunlight reemergent
over Sulphur; seasons; seasons of years; years; and the ranges' rhythms
started to be apparent too; the great long waves; the waves; the waves

the wave lap   wave lap   wave lap   wave lap   wave lap on the shore

blurred   and   blurring

the thrice held   trice   the trace of

vision's intermingling indistinctions

beyond

the glassbrick window

is the terrace
its flagstone walk, caraganas
borders trimmed with sweet elyssum deer won't eat
larkspur, pale blue and purple, lavender and sky, delphinium
and bumblebeed and hummingbirded
margins of dandelions—poor man's gold—tuffeting
the lawn beside the once-was cabin now garage
and o so neat pineappleweed

(O, I am for those patterns Fibonacciward
(O, O in the order spiraled pineappleweed)

The spruce trees, trees so anciently green
they look as if they've always been there,
been nailed into for corral posts for Peyto's packhorses
        (". . . when Bill Peyto and Jack Sinclair
        ("had the place where your Archives is now . . ."
        (thus Jimmy Simpson, saying it was
        ("the time I saw him make that violin . . ."
        (Jack Sinclair, that is,
        ("went over to Dave White's store
        ("got himself one of those round, wooden cheese boxes . . .
        ("you remember the type of boxes Stilton cheeses used to come in?
        ("Fixed it up and sat down and played it;
        ("had a right good tone, too.")
and I remember reading years later Marianne Moore in "An Octopus"
quoting Walter D. Wilcox's description of Bill Peyto
and realizing, for the first time,
poetry could be about "here" and not "anywhere else,"
and thus could be about "here" and "everywhere else."

Bill Peyto's Cabin: rough-hewn like himself,
placed by the lot's remoter edge, nearer the water,
as far away as he could be and it, yet near enough.
Jack Sinclair packed with Peyto, and prospected;
and when the Boer War came they flipped a coin,
Peyto won the toss and defended the Empire;
while Sinclair stayed in Banff and held the claim,
Peyto rode his horse before the enemy's lines
to draw their fire. After the war was over
Bill came home; and wandering Jack, from Coolgardie
decided to move on and find a fortune in the goldfields
agreeing that my grandfather could buy his lease.
Some five or six years later Jack, who failed to make a fortune,
wrote from an orchard he was working on,
inquiring if his old shack still stood,
and that's the last we hear of Jack
except in Whymper's papers where the cranky Englishman
deplores the actions of his packers, Bill and Jack.

Bill came home and built a legend out of loneliness.
One day he wandered into town and at the butcher's
asked how much a steak two inches thick would cost.
The butcher named a price, and Bill agreed.
Well, after it was cut Bill asked him for some salt
and ate the three-pound slab of meat uncooked.

The Simpsons' place, where Mrs Simpson's sweltering kitchen
havened shortbread on an oilcloth table
and milk to swallow down with tales of Rob Roy:
it was just beyond Big Jim's old midden, or the Mount Royal's,
        (his a rubbish heap, and its a garbage dump);
the ant hill in the rotting stump;
the spruce trees in the loop both bears and brothers climbed;
the lawn, half-mowed by Steve who spoke Ukranian,
whose hands were mounds, whose rakish fedora always bore a ring of sweat,
        (lawn only to the caragana bush
        (beside the bench which had arrived one Hallowe'en;
        (beyond it was a field of buttercups and wayward asters,
        (marguerites and foxtails, bumblebees and chickadees);
thistles' prickles on the path to Pete'n'Catharine's
which, when running through the hose's spray, were another hazard;
the little tree by our house's corner I knew had grown with me;
the Indian Cabin,
        (it had been Peyto's once but Pete'n'Catharine moved it,
        (moved it from the River Road and settled it
        (where it would block the view of Simpsons',
        (and where the Bearspaws stayed while Pete'n'Catharine
        (painted portraits of them all);
Jack Sinclair's Cabin,
        (moved from Lynx Street down the hill;
        (my father sawed one end out, put in folding doors,
        (making it a garage;
        (before that Quig—Doctor Quigley—
        (lived there a winter, lived in sin,
        (to my very Presbyterian grandmother's deep chagrin);
the carriage shed,
where Perella must have waited patiently for harness,
which Sammy turned into a shop;
near there, and scattered in the spruce,
the elk would lie on winter nights,
their heads like barren branches of leaflorn bushes,
their bodies forming frosty bodyprints in the snow;
the chickencoops which demands had turned to flats,
and one of them now held the Packard;

Pete'n'Catharine's home of logs;
and uphill from it where the Stockands lived until the war's end,
when Mildred and the boys moved in
    (and where one day when Billy and I had stolen paint
    (from underneath the Simpsons' porch
    (and swashed the concrete of our house a Kelly green,
    (we fled across the paths and roads
    (and persuaded Mildred we were playing hide'n'seek
    (and hid ourselves beneath the stormdoor basement staircase door);
the spruce tree hedge along both Lynx and Bear that Papa planted,
pruned and thickened to a density forbidding light;
the rose thorn bramble through which the three trails branched:
    to school by way of Mom's yellow stucco bungalow,
    up the ancient river bank where Dietz and Dave had engineered
    a tunnel in the river sand
    that went back sixty feet or more
    and Mom was terrified that one of Ike's cayuses would collapse
    the turf and we'd be buried,
    and we built dams with mud and hauled the hose uphill
    and filled the reservoirs
    into which we'd introduced first ladyfingers
    but building up progressively to blockbusters
    which we'd light and watch the mayhem in the little towns
    we had constructed downstream;
    to overtown from off the driveway,
    past Mrs Simpson's honeysuckles on the corner of their lot;
    and lastly from the porch and up the bank,
    directly past the barbecue of gravity-held bricks,
    (we didn't call it "barbecue," we called it "let's cook outside")
    and by the poplars and the wild roses to the street
    where later, when l was eight, and after Friday Cubs,
    I had to walk to the darkened house,
    and just before I got there,
    only the naked aspen woods to walk down through, but hesitant,
    a rotund bearling ambled out from underneath the compound gate
    and crossed the street and used **our path,**
    and in the darkness I knew he waited and awaited me:

more threatening	dark	it is	to pursue
a threat	into	the	darkness
than to	pursue	mere	darkness

the gravel driveway, source of stones, a glacier-gravel mix
of quartzites, stones with banded calcite,
black stones which gleamed when spat upon,
stones of mauve, deep purple, and rusty quartz,
smooth stones which streams had polished,
rough stones broken into barbs and jaggedness:

scabs	scars	kneepatch	badges
tumbles	falls	accidents	collisions
not wounds	like	Taffy's	scratches

and finally the street, Bear Street,
    (drawn to my attention ultimately
    (it's unusual for streets to have the names of animals;
    (letters came to Bayer, Baher, Baer, and Bare,
    (Behr, and Bier, and Bair, infrequently to Bear)
edged by the spruce of Papa's hedge,
its dark recesses and its secret passageways,
the street.

Beyond	the yard	the place	the street
far beyond	river	stories	relatives
accumulating	density	perception	places

the blurred	background	further	away

        the mountains

        the Rockies

        the world

        was never

        horizontal:

the hill the ancient river bank provided could impel me into spills,
the driveway's slope provided impetus to wagon rides or sleds,
where we built dams and blew them up we skied at Christmastime,
and where "let's cook outside" was in the undercut we hid,
spring meltwater ran in rivulets to puddle in the loop,
and bicycles scuffed brake marks in the gravel and the dust.

In the stillness

after voices cease

thought's force brims

(meniscus)

into   the temples'   furling   pressure

tension   binding   emotion   skating

as it were

on the bounded undersurface

(surface, however thin, two surfaces still a molecule apart,
(a point thick only, an infinity of points long and wide,
(however long, however wide)

the

infinite

surface

divides

an upperness

a lowerness:

light	ecstatic	circling
essence	ego	rainbow
ascendence	loss	spectre
upwardness	the	myself
convergence	airiness	my
rarefication	of	shadow
integration	pursuit	dancing
atemporality	thematic	in
silence	of	banked
greyness	romantic	clouds
silence	themes	beyond
time loss	agony	benighting
disintegration	in	eastern
chaos	plunging	vault
divergence	into	as
downwardness	pits	night
falling	of	looms
absolute	despair	gathering
essence	falls	darkness

spirits

suffusing

peaks

atop

mountains

far

brilliant

toward

slopes

climbing

exercises

the

lank

muscles

throughout

corporeal

density

into

death

soul

silvering

transparent

becomes

which

slope

to

way

gives

ground

drops

and

valleys

seem

despondent

thickening

into

blackening

fogs

whiteness

yielding

lead

the

take

me

beside

ghost

pale

grim

as

ghastly

fear

dragging

gravity

pulling

relentlessly

shallowing

downwards

Revelation
carves
from
air
the
puns,
the
kennings
patterns
of
what
carved
itself
in
thought
as
sculptors
translate
time
and
space
and
make
them
something
solid,
the
architecture
of

Sometimes
a
thought
or
quip
or
joke,
a
whisper,
speech,
or
utterance,
no
matter
how
obvious,
apparently
conceals
beneath
itself
what
it
depends
upon,
the
layered
awareness
of
its

I
know
it
seems
the
usual
cliché,
but
foreshortening
suggests
at
times
the
whole
rough
pile
of
scree
will
fall
upon
us,
silly
as
it
is
to
think
a

thought as something of a façade, and what we hope is whole but never can quite integrate with memory, the iceberg consciousness that makes our concepts deeper than imagination

dependence on the grottoes, caves, and caverns we in ancient days were lodgers in, the mind's concealments, archetypes, the fire an anodyne to darkness and the cave's bright eye

mountain lacks a foundation and is merely propped up by some sort of false-front brace, and is merely there to hide the struts and gimcracks holding it up

Attend
attenuance
a call to mind
accumulates

Thus: a boundary   of perception

      perceiving   and   perceived

                            membrane thin

                              (or thick)

less than thin   on the verge

                            always

of tearing   ripping

                 letting its contained perceptions

                            spill

           contaminate and flame contagions

spillway   damburst   flashflood   fury

                   spate and terror

               throughout the universe:

so: when voice is silent   manner and style spill

                           will

never be regained   nor sealed

                 dispersal's vapours

cloud   accumulate

as in a chilling   the recognitions   cognitions
               (anger in danger deserving)
                    endangered

and deranged   dismembered   torn

and the membrane   meniscus   overbrimmed

it is:
           not stillness spilled
but is:
           the skin of thought scraped off,
           the raw mind flensed
           as quick blood flows and pale flesh dims

till	all	**the**	lake	surface	**shimmering**	breaks
bottom	**branches**	**disappear**	**in**	reflected	glacier	**opacity**
reflected	**glacier**	disappears	in	Monet-	like	shimmering
only	an	impression	**like**	**glass-**	brick	**shattering**
		fell				

         the Rockies

bright range: **bearing:**

              :story
              :burden
              :the valueless
              :the invaluable
              :the light
              :north
              :by northwest
              :a shining in the west
              :scene and aspect
              :act and motive
              :time, mystery, language
              :recalcitrance
              :force
              :the shape of force
              :silence

              and

lake   :   lake bottom   :: | :   reflection

(suggestions   (of syllogism   endlessly) reflecting)

            ::   brow   :   mind

            ::   broken bowl   :   rim

            ::   form   :   idea

            ::   substance   :   essence

            ::   world   :   cosmos

            ::   a life   :   a history

            ::   a moment   :   eternity

            ::   personality   :   humanity

each   analogy   explicating   implicit   analogues   of   surface:

child's mind,   innocence in nature,   the feral and ferocious; so:

five years old,
growing in a sense of tininess
mountains ceasing to be *skena,* the zenith *proskena*

backdrop

Was it then?   At Lake Louise?

(not the postcard Lake Louise, but the place I had not yet been to, seen)

We have continually
to distinguish
occasion of place from place,
and cannot tell
if our first intimations of
infinity
eternity
reflections thereupon
came from within ourselves or
from a first visit to Tommy Armstrong's
barber shop
its mirrors parallel
reflections cannonading into darkening
distance
falling down and bending further down
until I thought that we must disappear
down its long funnel
into the shrinking world
of the Quaker Oats gentlemen
Dutch Cleanser ladies
Mary Jane and Sniffles
(oh, magic words of poof poof piffles)

We have continually
to distinguish
occasion of place from place,
and cannot tell
if our first intimations of
infinity
eternity
reflections thereupon
came from within ourselves or
from a first visit to Tommy Armstrong's
barber shop
its mirrors parallel
reflections cannonading into darkening
distance
falling down and bending further down
until I thought that we must disappear
down its long funnel
into the shrinking world
of the Quaker Oats gentlemen
Dutch Cleanser ladies
Mary Jane and Sniffles
(oh, magic words of poof poof piffles)

We have continually
to distinguish
occasion of place from place,
and cannot tell
if our first intimations of
infinity
eternity
reflections thereupon
came from within ourselves or
from a first visit to Tommy Armstrong's
barber shop
its mirrors parallel
reflections cannonading into darkening
distance
falling down and bending further down
until I thought that we must disappear
down its long funnel
into the shrinking world
of the Quaker Oats gentlemen
Dutch Cleanser ladies
Mary Jane and Sniffles
(oh, magic words of poof poof piffles)

And now I cannot isolate it from the postcard Lake Louise.

Two tour bus drivers, Rocky Mountain Tours boys, students,
roomed with us that summer (one of them Bob Kroetsch's cousin),
took me along for my first mountain climb (mountain? climb?),
Fairview, from the lake's edge by the trail to Saddleback,
and thence from Saddle Col and cabin to the summit cairn.

> How could Walter Wilcox say of Dave White's trail,
> from creek to lake and Saddleback beyond,
> "It is the worst trail I have ever seen"
> when from the fell woods of 1894 there was but it?
> These are sorts of paternosters.

Dark, ancient woods, lichen-hung with Old Man's Beard
and toadstooled, cool, damp, and musty, the rich blush
of swift mountain summer's ripening and rot,
pleat-folded seasons, fell of germination in the duff:
we walked the angling rise of switchbacks upwards,
the way as ancient as the trees, imagining the print
of moccasin in dampened soil, older than trees.

> A first fishing shack by the shore, 1890,
> from trees felled by the lake, Dave White again,
> described its details later on, after his marriage,
> to his father-in-law, John Donaldson Curren,
> so he could paint it, since it had burned down
> in 1891, otherwise quite unrecorded.

Across the avalanche paths, remnants of snow in the thwarts,
emerging to the sun, suddenly our noses sense the differences
of ripening and maturing: what is rotting, what is not,
from the dank, the childhood forest, its toad-world warm and mildew,
to the dry maturing, dusty fronds of grasses, waving in the sun,
tussocks by the boulders where we sat and appled.

> In 1889 George and William Vaux, their sister Mary,
> photographers all three, her demoiselle friend, Mary Sharples,
> (my grandmother's sister's sister-in-law, a "cousin aunt")
> from Philadelphia and Quakers all, rode atop a boxcar
> into steam and wood-ash and a wonder of sensation
> all the way from Morley up to Laggan.

A sorting of the past, a sort of past, sorteeing a past,
and past the marmot-whistled, pika-squealing fellfield,
lichen, tufts of goathair on the rocks' sharp edges,

the last larch far below, and Sheol's bright blackness beckoning,
by zigzags and the trail in dust diminuendoes disappears;
we reach the broad-swept circle of the peaks, the summit.

      The linguist, man of maths, the polymathic Charles Fay,
      the Swiss Guides' "Chipmunk" and climber, Dr. or Professor,
      (somewhere I have a note that shows he also is
      (quite distant kin), was also, 1894, a first precursor
      one who made this slight, albeit meaningful, ascent.

We walk the steps, the trail, the path toward the sky,
while I, an atavist, precede the trail by twenty years
will lead me to an aged unicorn at these bare heights,
a poor old one-horned goat who'll linger here
among the ragged clouds, November cirrus, 1971,
but then in '51 I did not know I walked among the duff
and moulder of the trees that Papa felled, the dust.

    It is not the tininess   of the waterskimmers on the lake,
                                ourselves upon the peak's immensity,
                                or the model railroad people at the pass,
    but is the hugeness   both of the deepened course of glaciers,
                                and the peaks which ring the blue-cloud tarn,
    which suddenly makes time visible   its passage apparent in the cliffs.

Fell of fabric   fold of time

the railroad   pared back

earlier
wandering men
come across the pass
one of them hurt

they hunger   they stumble

in gaunt fear   and   hunger is companion

the Stoneys provide food

dramatis personae are all dead

Years after, seventy or more, Pete and Catharine, painting William Twin:
his eyes closing as he draws pictures from his past,
his mind not dozing.   They ask him questions as they paint:

"Who were . . . who was the first white man you saw? When was that?"

            His wrinkled cheeks,
            his hands' crenellated knuckles,
            mind's mattering battlements,
            iron fell's fells,
            his fingers stretching in the strings of air;
            he puts down the rifle they had borrowed for a prop;
            his picturing place wanders
            from studio to a paintbrush-flowering glen
            William and his twin brother, Joshua, are playing in when
            they meet the strangers, strange white men,
            the first he'd seen.

            His visage innocence becomes
            the ten-year old child he is,
            their camp near where the pipestone is,
                  the rivers flow together.

            His there-then mind recalls
            a fragment buried in the soil of change:

                  These men come hungry
                  from a place
                  where people do not go;

                  one of them hurts,
                  dazed beyond his hunger

            and William sees the man's line pain
            while he reclines against a tree and eats.

Little else:

            he makes the signs:

                  pipestone (by mannering its matter)

the rivers merging, "Pipestone" and "Cold-Water River"

an indentation at his brow, his temple

the sunken cheeks

and then:

in quick small taps he pats his head

curls his fingers in a clamp
and clasps his fleshy nose within

looks down

blades his hand at solar plexus

repeats the pats, the clamp of nose.

Passage vanishes.
He sits back again,
his story told.

Pete and Catharine work silently at painting him,
his closing eyes, silent in thought,
inside the story they have seen.

Inside another silence, and leagues remote, another wandering mind:

madness, memory chaotic, maelstrom of speechlessness, confusion
of wapta, washmawapta, waputik, hungabee,
yukness, odaray, opabin and oesa, wiwaxy,
minnestimma, minewakun, and wastach,
the ascension of heejee, nom, yamnee,
tonsa, sapta, shappee, sagowa,
saknowa, neptuak, wenkchemna,
nouns and numbers in Waesgebee
Samuel Allen learned in a summer in paradise
he and others spent near where Twin had met Hector
and placed on the landscape
two years before the mist of madness slunk 'round his mind.

Sam Allen's silence, like Twin's,
pictures without utterance the past.

But then?

"What do you call it?" pointing:
Allen's forefingers point up and away from his temples,
he draws his fingers like dripping rain or dribbling spittle
    down his chin,
stands his two first fingers of his right hand
on his lowered left thumb, and then
prance-capers his slender fingers up the cliffs
    the knuckles form to the little finger's prominence.

And then Twin says, "Waputik."

Allen points to two bright, moving spots of snow,
a faint line across the scree above a cliff, and
"Waputik," he repeats.

Twin smiles and nods, says, "Waputik."

Time is a leaf of gold that does not tarnish,
    a wire of gold drawn fine,
    a ductile line attenuated that ultimately breaks.

Twin scorned Wilcox—"White man no good eyes"
when the white man's fieldglasses revealed but one goat
    and Twin's eyes saw a herd,

but Wilcox praised him:
    "a fine-looking Indian . . .
    "nearer to a realisation of the fine ideal . . .
    "such as one sees on coins . . .
    "than almost any savage's I have ever seen."

	Twin	Hector	Vauxes	White	Sharples	Allen	Wilcox	Fay	Whyte

Hector: stumbles near starvation;

Vauxes: photographers all three;

White: builds a log cabin;

Sharples: vows never to sleep in wilderness again;

Allen: learns words and names, goes mad;

Wilcox: subsumes Allen's names and applies his own;

Fay: in the days to come a climber;

Whyte: Peter and Catharine paint William and history recapitulates.

Twin tells Wilcox of his wife, four sons—all dead of smallpox:

"Me sleep no more now
"all time think me
"squaw die, four papooses die
"no sleep me
"one little boy, me
"love little boy, me
"little boy die,
"no longer want to live, me"

And all by which means touch our past

lustre and fanning:

ember   remember

glow   spark   gleam

brighten   against darkness   embodying

flare   glimmering   memory

tinder   into   flame

flicker   the   twigs   to   brilliance

puffs   breath   toward   gathering   warmth

wards   gloom   off   keeps   flames

growing   sticks   hearth   and   heats

mouldering   memories   alive   in   the   minds   of   ourselves   after

the   past   has   started   to   seem   a   chimærical   dance   of   fire

and then

All that is fell   **is brightness**

Letter to Mary Townsend Sharples Schäffer Warren

"You couldn't ask for quieter neighbours,"
you used to tell my mother,
speaking of the graveyard's citizens
across Learn's Hill from your place, Tarry-a-While.
I find myself more frequently looking for their addresses
and yours, as if to post them letters, tell them things,
account for what we're doing day to day and year to year.
Accounting or recounting? I read the other day
accounting goes the other way: we borrow from the Earth
our children's use of it. I think you'd understand.
You gave us better than we're handing on, I think,
but we are learning, albeit slowly.
You'd be surprised to see what's being made of you:
a book, a reprint of your *Old Indian Trails* we made anew
with colour reproductions of the lantern slides
you so long ago quite lavishly hand-coloured,
appended with your heretofore unpublished text
about the mapping and the exploration of Chaba Imne;
an exhibition of your works with large-size photos
Ed derived by Cibachrome from those same lantern slides;
and there is talk of turning you into a movie,
the babble of the brook of gossip suggesting
who better could be found than Jane Fonda
to play your robust, quite intriguing self;
your self the shells of myth are circling wider,
and you start to grow, expand, become a wider set
of meanings, markings, unlimitations;
it may be what you thought you'd like to be
when you suggested you were on the subject
of these mountains an encyclopaedia.
Sometimes I wonder about the hedges on your yard:
the imposition of a sense of order
on untrammeled nature, the hedges are so alien
to everything you came to love by what you meant
when you said "garden."

My Garden,
you declared,
is neither raked nor hoed.
It has no signs prohibiting loitering;
sprinkler and fertilizer are alien to it;
it juxtaposes   colours   in combinations
the eyes of horticulturalists would
consider   madness.

It is an
ordered wildness.

Pasque Flowers and Spring Beauty,
nodding blues of the campanulates,
the tiny orchids, Fly-spotted, Coral Root,
the shyly tonsured Drummond's Dryas,
the brilliant orange of Western Wood Lilies,
small flaming Shooting Stars,
the slippers of Calypso stepping,
the greyish-yellow of Wolfwillow blooms,

an ordered wildness

in

contradistinction to
your parrot's
wild disorderedness in
reciting, "Where, o where has my little dog gone"
"Go on! Go on!"
which he, of course, added on.

I like to think of your splendid jest, so happily played out
upon your eastern relatives who so much wanted, sans effort,
to emulate your summers on the trail,
and so you gave them a pack trip three days long
that took them deep into the mountains.
A whole morning of preparing, watching wranglers, packers getting ready,
tying diamond hitches, heaving loads,
and fitting out the dudes with boots and chaps and hats,
before the line of horses sauntered slowly from the stable,
easing   up   the road toward the big hotel and past it,
then cut down through pine forest ***off the trail,***
and having on occasion to spur their horses over deadfall,
duck sweeping branches, they all loved it.
By the river they stopped to check the ford
before their guide decided it was safe
and plunged his horse into the boiling current.
It took the afternoon to get them all across,
and then they rode downstream and turned the mountain's corner
while their guide looked carefully about to find a place for camp.
The following day, an hour wasted searching for the horses,
they had to cross the river by an island
and then rode a glacially deposited ridge beside the strange formations,
picked out a safe way to descend and crossed the railroad tracks
and made their way quite carefully along a creek
and to a lake where they made camp
and praised their lucky stars how fortunate they were.
On their third morning, fully in their confidence,
they made their preparations rapidly;
their guide had warned them it was miles they had to go
to get to Banff.

And so it was near dusk and twenty miles later
the pack string wearily approached the barns,
and none of your relatives the wiser
they had never been more than six or seven miles from town,
the horses spent their first night near the stable,
and the wranglers drank their nights away in Banff.
The only difficulty Warren had
was to keep from laughing and to try to make it seem so difficult.

I wonder what you'd think to see it all now opened up,
to cars, to casual visitors who wonder whether
they can make it up to Jasper and back in a day,
when scarce six weeks were adequate for you and Mollie.
They'll not accept the country was far better known
by you and your kind then, when the century began;
and it takes time to get to know anywhere quite well.

The less that's known of it, the better it can be known.
Those relatives who took the three days' packtrip around Tunnel
perceived it slowly and carefully, and knew the force of rivers
ere they were done, or else they had not gone.

Not that you would have complained about the roads too much:
you would have been the first to open up the windscreen,
to see and feel the wind fierce in your eyes
as you and Mary did when with her brothers
you came to the Rockies, riding on the boxcar roof
all the way from Morley up to Laggan.
(Did you ever apologize to William Twin
(for having him drive horses all the way up there
(so you could ride those last few miles, Laggan up to Lake Louise?)
There's just a jot of "Greenhorn!" in your relating
how uncomfortable it was to sleep on spruce bough beds
that first night in the wilderness
and vowing that you'd never sleep beneath the stars again.
Great irony that "Mary Schäffer," Philadelphian,
in later summers spent seasons on the trail,
regretting only "Civilisation and its Discontents"
eventually would replace the idylls of the quest.

George Fox felt God's grandeur quivering in himself,
but did not disavow the world therefore,
and knew subjective wilderness could reward;
a pre-Romantic notion of an Eden in America,
the prelapsarian wild Edward Hicks evoked
in gentle wilds where lion and lamb lay side by side;
how Peaceable a Kingdom.

If anything's to be made from Quaker thought
and how you came to be "a hunter of peace"
where cougar, grizzly, moose, and ram
in nature's equilibrium assort themselves,
then is it "The Peaceable Kingdom" thee was in search of?
Did, when the Endless Chain seemed to seek infinity,
thee contemplate its orderedness?
Awareness is a human trait,
like laughing, blushing, weeping,
and it seems to sire them
as it does awe, respect, and contemplation, sense of loss,
the ranged meanings we—and thee—ascribe
to wilderness and lives examined,
"endless chain"?

Inner light
radiant suffusion

illuminating   darkness
words   blanketing
telling   everything
tolling   lives

Panther Falls
Ka-toon-da Tinda

windy   plains

Chaba Imne

the rapture

the ecstasy

Thy husband died, and thee was left alone;
his botany unfinished thee took up, completed, published;
then, forsaking warnings, thee departed for the north,
the barely-sought-out trails of ranges north from Laggan,

hunting peace

only in the high places

were he   and thee

together

Some notes and explanations

The ripples begin where I begin; they wash up on that larger circle, the world.

The lot, the neighbourhood, the milieu, the family, the town, the community, the ring of mountains containing the Bow Valley first, then the greater ranges of the Rockies beyond, the national parks of the continental crest: these are the expanding—the receding—horizons of consciousness "Some Fittes and Starts" involves.

One who chooses to write about his neighbourhood should select it carefully. The spirits of ancient Banff (1883–1914) took up residence in our backyard before I was born. I met them before I knew who they were.

Bill Peyto, the Rockies' most illustrious guide and outfitter, built a rough shack on the grounds where the grazing was good and the Bow River was near. His prospecting and packing partner Jack Sinclair, a western Australian from Coolgardie, had been an ore seeker in Bulolo, New Guinea, before he reached the Rockies about 1890. Jack's cabin was more substantial and better contructed than Bill's. At the outbreak of the Boer War Bill and Jack flipped a coin to see who would defend the Empire. Bill won the toss, and in South Africa he rode his horse before enemy lines to draw their fire, inducing them to disclose their locations. After the war he returned to Banff, whereupon Jack, who had tended the claim in Bill's absence, decided to seek his fortune in gold fields of the Transvaal. His arrangement with my grandfather resulted in our family's establishment on the property between Bear Street, Lynx Street, and the river. Nextdoor was Jimmy Simpson, an English expatriate who "fell in with 'the boys of Banff'", and became a trapper and hunter in his winters, an outfitter and guide in his summers. He also became Banff's first art collector. Jim was no spirit; he was very much alive, a spritely seventy or so, when I was a kid. Tom Wilson, a man from Barrie, Ontario, who had arrived with the railroad survey crews in 1881, and stayed behind in Banff to become the first entrepreneurial spirit engaged in outfitting pilgrims, was Jim's first employer.

Mrs Simpson, very Scottish, was a constant source of oatcakes and Caledonian heritage. She was at the centre of artistic life in Banff, involved in theatre and reading circles, vigorously engaged in figure skating. (The Simpson daughters, Margaret and Mary, had a world career in skating in the 1930s.)

Across the street were two embodied fantasies. Ike Mills' Riding School was the ostentatious name of a horse rental stable where the remittance man from Robin Hood Bay swaggered and staggered in practical-joking manner. Once a world champion dogracer, a master of masquerade, Ike was terror incarnate and fascination. Ike's persistent threat, frequently realized, was to headfirst a kid into the manure box, then order him home to tell his mother he needed a bath. Alma Mills was a delicate New Englander with French Canadian roots who had been a 'cellist in a ladies' trio which performed at the Banff Springs Hotel where she met and fell in love with Ike. Alma served me my first glass of beer when I was about five. She kept chickens. Next to Ike's was the government building where each morning labourers assembled. Inside the building was an inferno of scattering sparks, Steve Hope's smithy shop.

In the family were Bubby (Barbara), Dave, and Harold, my sister and brothers. Up the hill—an ancient bank of the Bow River, truth to tell—beyond the cave Dave and Harold dug in the sandy soil with Dietz, a neighbourhood kid, and others, was *Mom's* my paternal grandmother's residence. *Mom* and *Papa,* Dave White, married in the last year of Victoria's reign. Their home was a darkness of Victorian bric-à-brac, glass lampshades, tasseled curtains, feather pictures and figurines. Mom's father was John Donaldson Curren, a Scottish Presbyterian coal seeker and coal miner. He died a year to the day before I was born: I am ultimately named for him. *(Jon* without an *h, Whyte* rather than *White;* a later volume of *The Fells of Brightness* may explain these anomalies.)* John Curren is now esteemed as an early naive painter of Rocky Mountain historical subjects and landscapes, their spanking green forests summoning a Rocky Mountain Eden.

Of uncles who lived nearby, Clifford, the oldest, married Mildred, and they had three sons, Cliff, Donald, and Peter. Peter, the nextborn, married Catharine Robb, and they became *Pete'n'Catharine,* living a hundred yards north of us in a log house, another source of cookies, meringues, ginger ale and grapefruit juice, conversation and the best library in town. They met at art school in Boston and were painters of portraits and landscapes. Lila, the aunt, married Cameron Stockand, and they lived in the neighbourhood with their kids until I was four.

Between our house and *Pete'n'Catharine's* was my grandfather's old carriage shed where Perella had her stall. In the late 1940s it became *Sammy's Shop*, where Sam Ward, an irrepressible tease, a master carpenter, a constant entertainer, was willing to suffer the interruptions of an inquisitive little kid.

It was a well-chosen neighbourhood.

A few other names: Bill Peyto packed for Walter D. Wilcox in the 1890s. (Marianne Moore quotes Mr Wilcox on Bill Peyto in "An Octopus". Her poem showed me the breadth of subject matter my neighbourhood could encompass.) Mr Wilcox and his friend Samuel E.S. Allen explored the Lake Louise region in 1893–1894. Mr Wilcox was a superior photographer. Mr Allen was a linguist and spirited climber. The better namer, Samuel Allen fell into dementia praecox shortly after his summer of joy in the Rockies in 1894; the affliction forestalled his defense of his toponomy on the summit crest of the Rockies; hence Walter Wilcox's names adorn most of the features they competitively named.

The Vauxes were dedicated Victorian visitors. Photographers, Philadephians, Quakers, amateur glaciologists, the brothers William and George, and their sister Mary, visited the Rockies first in 1887; their descendents still consider the Rockies and the Selkirks a playground for wildland recreation and intellectual and artistic pursuit. Mary Vaux's teenage friend Mary Sharples was a wildflower painter and photographer. Twice married, her first husband, Charles Schäffer, was kin of my maternal grandmother. In 1931 my mother visited her *Aunt Mary* and her second husband, Billy Warren, in Banff, where she met my father. Mary Sharples Schäffer Warren was Banff's first resident writer. Dr Charles Fay, a major early climber in the Rockies and Selkirks, is so distant a relative his kinship is of less importance than his prose which, in *Appalachia*, recounts so much of the history of early alpinism in the Rockies.

—Jon Whyte

THE FELLS *of* BRIGHTNESS, VOL. 2: WENKCHEMNA
Preface

To clear up the major difficulty of the volume, the second of five which in total become *The Fells of Brightness,* "wenkchemna" is Stoney for ten. I have used the ten peaks of the Moraine Lake region, familiar to all Canadians as the twenty-dollar bill, as eidolons for the last ten fittes of *Wenkchemna.* Samuel E.S. Allen of Philadelphia named them by their numerals in 1894, but the departures of the poem reflect their renaming.

A few other sources: the big-linguistic matter in "Sagowa" comes from the entry "join" in Eric Partridge's *Origins.* and from "The Animals of the Burgess Shale" by Simon Conway Morris and H.B. Whittington, an article which appeared in *Scientific American,* July, 1979. S.E.S. Allen's account of his traverse of Wastach, Wenkchemna, and Opabin passes appeared in *The Alpine Journal,* in 1896–97, and Dr Charles Fay's description of Philip Abbot's accident, "The Casualty on Mount Lefroy," appeared in *Appalachia* in 1896. Dr Fay's "The Mountain as an Influence in Modern Life" appeared in *Appalachia,* Vol IX, 1905, 29. Miss Gertrude Benham's notes on the ascent of "Hiji," or Mount Fay, appeared in *Alpine Journal,* Volume XXII, p.333. Lovers of recondite lore may be interested to know Charles Fay was uncle to Hazel Sutton Hawkeshurst, wife of Harold Hawkeshurst, my great uncle, brother to my grandmother, Florence Carpenter. It seems information too good to lose, too abstruse to include anywhere else.

Jon Whyte

ECHO
ECHO
ECHO
ECHO
ECHO

Sapta

Peak V, 3053 metres, 10018 feet, First ascent 1927, H.F. Ulricher and companion

Intelligibility distinguishes a difference
between
the Earth's intelligent   the Earth's intelligence
a morpheme and

isolating
a sound

a world of difference

The Earth's intelligible because we share
with annelids, cyclops, elephants, bacteria
a tumor on the spine we call a brain?

The Earth intelligible before
intelligence sensed it,
before sensing all the world's bounty,
making sense of it,
                              it provided sense
                              sensation
                              the sensational

And what's unfound is confoundingly unfounded

hence arguments often fail.

Peaks lacking intelligence
contribute to the Earth's intelligence.

Think, for a moment, on an unmountained Earth.
Uninterrupted plains of low relief,
the weather of the place:
dessicating wind, no rills of surface forming clouds,
little rain, snow only in arctic regions,
yet colder winters everywhere and hotter summers;
few lakes, few streams, no rivers except in the north
for almost all—with those exceptions—rise in mountains.
Vegetation only on the shores of oceans.

The intelligence mountains yield the Earth.

Think on Sapientia or Cybele,
wisdom womening Earth,
Gaea, Kore, Psyche, Echo, Iris,
in the grand grace of the world,
fecundity, soil, source,
the unkempt world in wild state,
the gentleness of high streams' song
Oreads on dancing feet come skippering on scree,
bend light, break avalanche,
cry in the wind-cries in the pass,
and bless bare rock in beauty.

Neptuak

Peak IX, 3236 metres, 10617 feet, First ascent, 1902, J. Norman Collie, Hugh E.M. Stutfield, George M. Weed, Hermann Wooley, Christian Kaufmann

Utter what we will—utter:
sharp, filmy, absolute, pure, bright, steep, near—
as a sharpened lithic fragment;
or, more deeply, sheer.

Sinister talon, cloud-snagging nail,
glittering, threatening, sharp
Neptuak cleaves into brilliance, parting the air.
Of the ten fangs that shade here, Neptuak's canine,
graceful, intriguing, sharp-witted, quick.

Terror attend her, sunlight befriend her,
rebirth of Earth-spirit grace her
breaking from shadow, pale clouds about her,
white light veiling her face.
Let thick mist abound here, surround her and swirl,
sacrifice bursting from Earth
in radiant ritual,
refracting skies' glory, crystalline tor.

Shade's darkness, her rumpled robe, lies at her feet,
she yearns and reaches to the sky.

Perpetuates herself, turning in air,
fronded and flickering ice-dragon's tongue,
fog in sundogs of mist.

Anxious, isolate weather brimmer,
the cauldron of cloud below black,
wimpled in snow, wuthering higher,
brimmed on the cusp of Wenkchemna-Neptuak.

From the barren col Neptuak signs death's division,
piercing the Earth's thin web of life,
the arrowpoint diversion,
the tangling of storm,
the rankling rush of fur against knife.

Wenkchemna

Peak X, 3173 metres, 10411 feet, First ascent, 1923, F.C. Bell, A.W. Drinnan, H. Herriot, T.B. Moffatt, Mrs R. Neil, Miss E. Thompson, R. Williams, Christian Hasler

IMPASSE
IMPASSION
IMPASSIONATELY
PASSIONATELY
PASSIONATE
COMPASSION
PASSION
PASS
PASSE
PASSES
ENCOMPASSES
COMPASSES
PASSES

PASS			PASSING			SURPASS
PASSING	:	FANCY	::	FANCYING	:	PASSION
RATIONAL	:	PASSION	::	PASSIONATE	:	RATION
		RATIO	:	RATIOCINATION		
		PASS	:	AGES		

PASSAGES
PASSAGE

(All of the above, none of the above, if without love)

Way rocky, wind ragging the clouds,
first snow falling, winter's last snow still unmelted,
last larches passed, slide roar beyond us,
we pick our path by zigzag angles upward,
wondering whether this hike's worth doing,
or if oromania afflict us.

                    Wenkchemna: path, pass, peak—
                    permanence behind transparency,
                    permanence, the ghost of hope, solidity,
                    for Earth's forces felt inform morphology.

        Sullen in dull attitude;
          grey, the null of place we stray in;
            silent the lull of what wind whying
what means   mull we   what pleasure's here
   as weary foot falls on footpath
                          wind wrath
              calls us
              pull arms in for warmth
as storm seems truncheon of winter nearing.

   cloud   **shroud**
        opaque   **awake**
              trail   avail
                 hidden   **veils**
                           time
                  until   winds
              tatter   frenzy
        c l e a r s   a w a y
   a   w a y   t o w a r d   t h e   p a s s

Hands jam pockets; head bends, avoiding wind;
misery, each switchback's bend into blast
driven from pass into summer-softened faces.

Desolation   Consolation
        Wilcox   named
                these   valleys
                        barrens   fellfields
                              unforgiving
                    relentless   glaciers
              the peaks   surrounding
          masked   summits
perenially   eroding

"Look at that: last year's snow's not even melted;
"and not a breath of autumn interfering
"with winter's onset. Wilcox and Peecock were stormed in too,
"weren't they? August?" "Yes, but they didn't come this way.
"Wouldn't have made it, but they proceeded up
"to Consolation, lakes, valley, pass. Named it 'Consolation'
"since they thought this 'Desolation.'
"Proper name today. Never more desolate,
"all of it I can see; no more than you."

"Allen named it 'Wenkchemna'?" "I'm not so sure he named
"the pass. Named 'Opabin,' that's certain;
"I'd have to reread his articles
"to see what he named here. Must have been a better day than this.
"Terrific stuff all right, made it from Paradise
"over Wastach, over Wenkchemna,
"over Opabin, walked the moors, walked right back."

```
                    pass

      beckoned                               beyond
      birth                                  birth
      tension                                intention
      taut                                   taught
      col                                    call
      here                                   hear
      sight                                  site
      seen                                   scene
      placement                              place meant
      now                                    know
   stand under                            understand
      peak                                   peek
      wear                                   aware
      height                                 hight
      place        ____          plays
                  [    ]
  DRAWN           [ O ]      NWARD
                  [    ]
  DRAWN           [ I ]   ИWAЯᗡ
                  [    ]
                  [ see ]
                  [    ]
                  ........
                see      the
```

clouds   seethe   clouds in cauldron
whirling about us, the wind the whine of gods' exhalations
at the ring's break   the pass: **Wenkchemna** _____

Limestone—lifeless, rough-edged, fragmentary, friable rock—
the yielded product of long ages' life, the shells of animals,
the soft rain down of dying generations, the stuff of bone
which bears us, holds us up as it contained the pulpy stuff
of clams, crustaceans, animalculi sans skeletons.
In its greyness, in its water-pitted surfaces, small pools
recall the tidal depths where trillions of small animals
discarded shells in shoals, on reefs, on epeirogenic shores,
the sinking, bevelled beaches of Cretaceous ages,
the tropic edges of the continent, the inland Bearpaw Sea.

....

A day's brisk walk:	*History leads us astray:*
ease ruck, seek space,	*August, I recall,*
delve high beyond	*Allen started early,*
Paradise's limits:	*up the valley all the way*
how grand a route	*from lower Paradise,*
no path leads toward!	*crossed his Wastach,*
Bands of rock, a platform	*sojourned swiftly,*
steps, and bright Sagowa	*saw the notch of pass,*
sharply pointing upward,	*pressed on, dropped down,*
gnomon peak, and growing	*into the Eagle Eyries;*
as easefully I stride	*noted how another pass*
the gap, the great grey	*nicked on the north*
towers leaning away	*another way,*
and—ah!—a glimpsing eye	*sought it out,*
of lake peers up	*then reaching there,*
and sees stranger,	*turned about,*
the goat	*three passes later,*
who scrabbles inspiration,	*six in the day,*
sustenance from the barrens	*reaching his companions*
here beside the lake	*who blithely wondered*
and glaciers.	*what he'd seen.*

Crossing the Wastach
and Wenkchemna Passes,
I reached the level
of the rocky, desolate,
treeless valley beyond.
This I have called
Opabin, or rocky.
The descent from the
Wenkchemna Pass
into the Opabin Valley

"Let's do it!" Pamela
suggests, and I wonder
why not, we'll make it through
to O'Hara, I think,
in time for tea and the bus.
Wenkchemna's summit by trail
then 'David'-strides sliding
the scree slope of purple, grey,
green, pale green, glaucous rocks,
mauves, and dusty limestone

glittering quartzites streaked by rusty, bloody hues
ashen grey, iridescent skims of purple
hummingbirding, quetzaling quartzose,
ochre yellow and pale orange,
the glistening gravel of the scree in piebald hue:
pebbles, pobbles, cobbles, crabbles,
scrabbles, dibbles, dabbles,
daubs of colour, liver purple, kidney brown,
until

was over broken rock
and scree
Immediately below the pass
stood a tall limestone pillar,
serving as a good landmark
where to turn upward
on my return;
for from this side
the peaks of the watershed
are merely a succession
of tremendous walls,
all looking about alike,
so that it would be
not difficult to confuse them.

by the eyries' columns
I open two bottles of beer.
Scanning the glacier to the east
seeking a safe route up,
knowing we must press fast
and not idle,
seeing only a glacieret,
consider it easy, since Allen
found it so, as I recall.
Two steps by meadows
bring us to heaped moraines
small ponds, sunken mills
where we peer down to ice
into the slithering glacier.

As I advanced
up the snow troughs
by the side of the glacier's
lateral moraine,
I kept a continual look-out
for 'shooting' gullies
in the cliffs
which covered the vicinity
with debris.
At last I gained the glacier,
and it proved quite free
from crevasses.

The sun's heat has awakened
gravel slurries, water runnels,
streams cascading into crevasses,
ogives' circular cracks,
until we reach the bergschrund
(or randkluft? The big one.)
Pamela's in running shoes,
we have no rope, just hope,
it's only two o'clock;
once we reach the pass
it'll be swift descent
to tea, the bus, and back.

It was only 9:30,
and the sun's rays
had not yet reached
this part of the valley,
so vast were the walls
on either side.
The neve was,
therefore, coated
with the morning crust, and
as the slope was not steep,
except near the top,
I had no difficulty
in reaching the summit
of Opabin Col at 10 o'clock,
9000 ft. above the sea.

Icicles fangs in crevasse's maw
anthropomorphize fear and doubt
hesitating us
while we seek a safe route
in the tesselated
shifting plates of ice.
I think we might avoid the void
by climbing up around the ice
where slurries of gravel sliding
over deep blue-ice
scurrying down to another crevasse
raise new anxieties, but
a snow bridge links neve
to the ice banking Opabin Col.
4 o'clock: we're missing tea.

The transcendental function of a pass,
the whither which becomes a thither
in a moment but a scramble from crevasse
which dizzily we reach—a dither.

Before me I saw a broad valley,
destitute of vegetation,
and walled on either side,
by lofty, precipitous cliffs,
the glaciers at the feet
of which resembled
the dashing waves
of a stormy sea.
From my feet downward
swept the névé,
terminating
in a fine glacier below,
while two lakes appeared
in the rocky valley, which,
for the sake of uniformity,
I have known as the Opabin lakes.

To the left of the col
rose a gigantic peak,
or, more properly,
a 'peaked' wall,
which bids fair to occupy
a prominent place
as regards altitude
among the other mountains
of the region.

Beyond the glacier lay another,
steeper, slicker glacier
shadowed now by afternoon.
Going first, I slide into a rock
then tell Pamela I'll grab her.
"Hold on tight, Marie!"
to find us both skittering downward
in an icewater stream.
No hand held hand tighter than hers
mine as we traverse the cracks
and wonder just how big it is—
while, I recall for her
the day the British army lost
two soldiers in a crevasse
here for an hour or two.
She fails to find it reassuring.

The rock is warm
though sun has gone
beyond Biddle and chill winds
wave the drying saxifrage
and we draw hands' warmth from rock
reconsidering dinner
and if our high day's drawn
us out too long
and if we'll walk the road.

Hungabee's bright plumed chieftainship gleams
in the sun's obliquely falling rays,
Odaray's bold wedge a shadow seems,
darkness, blacks, deep greys.

I photographed
the surroundings,
desended the peak, névé,
and glacier leisurely,
and was travelling along
one of the snow-gullies
by the old moraine.
On reaching the top
of a rise of rock,
I looked down upon a herd
of eleven goats
lying or standing upon the snow
not 20 ft. away.
They did not remain long.

I watched the goats
as they climbed
the snow-slopes,
waiting their turn
to get upon the cliffs,
and making ample allowance
for stones
dislodged by their brethren,
until the last had disappeared
over the Wenkchemna Pass.

We walk trail where he walked
wilderness,
and yet Wiwaxy, which he named
for the wind flags bright
for us as it did for him.
Here's where the mouse
slept in Catharine's hair;
there's where the dozy poet slept;
now down by Sid Graves' trail,
its switchbacks cut too short
and, now it seems, too frequently
and there's where Harry Greenham
first met Margaret, the great trees
of that camp now rotting slowly.

The still green lake,
the smoke rising
from the lodge
where, we find,
the garbage truck can bear us
back to Hector, Laggan,
and I've never seen the Watchtower
more beautiful than by that last
light as we ride in the truckback
down the road.

Near here where Tommy met his apparitional Adeline
Jim Brewster slept as Charles Fay had bidden
after their success on Death-Trap Col;
often the route's been walked and ridden
Tranquillity ascends the Gorge of the Winds,
and Lake O'Hara's secrets are rehidden

Then I began to ascend slowly,
as the sun was hot,
and there was no water
upon this side of the pass.
I had completed
about three-fourths
of the ascent,
and was resting
among some large boulders,
when attracted by falling stones,
I espied two yellow objects
circling the ledges
to my left.
My glass revealed
two silver-tip bears,
who, scenting me,
stopped to investigate.
I did not move,
and, finally,
perhaps alarmed,
they turned around
and were soon out of sight
around the corner.
I then lost no time
in crossing the
Wenkchemna and Wastach Passes
to the tent,
and next day
(Sunday, August 12)
returned to Lake Louise.

Sundown now,
the car still at Moraine.
Postponing the dinner reservation,
we hitch the road, knowing
few cars will be headed in,
wondering whether we should walk
the last eleven kilometres,
meditating how fine a walker
Allen was, certainly better on ice
than we, when Pamela remembers
Anne Pedersen at Paradise Bungalows
whom I walk up the road to ask
and, mercifully, she's there.
Wondering which is madder:
to follow history's route
almost missing dinner,
or to have turned back at the pass
and never to have known what
thither was whithersoever
there
and turned around,
only to have glimpsed the eyrie
'round the corner.
We lost no time in getting
to the car and rounding Temple
back to the Post
for dinner
and that night
(Thursday, September 1, '83)
returned to Banff.

...rary of Canada

SEEN BY NLC

Bibliothèque nationale du Canada

VU PAR LA BNC

166